on

f   **ts:**

                    ed

Oral Communication Skills for Vo-Tech Students:

A Competency-Based Approach

Cathy Sargent Mester and Robert T. Tauber

Prakken Publications, Inc.

© 1991 by Prakken Publications, Inc.
P.O. Box 8623
Ann Arbor, MI 48107

Library of Congress Catalog Card No. 91-60165
ISBN: 0-911168-79-6

Designed by Sharon K. Miller

Acknowledgments

This book is the result of years of discussions with many individuals involved in vocational-technical education. It is not possible to list them all here, but several key groups and individuals must be singled out and given special appreciation for their contributions to our work. First, we thank the entire staff of the Erie County Technical School in Erie, Pennsylvania. Their graciousness in allowing us to study and observe their classrooms, coupled with the inspiration derived from their concerns about their students' communication training, was the single greatest factor in starting this project. Second, we thank all of those professionals who have shared their thoughts with us in writing so that we can then share them with you in Section IV. We are further indebted to two great proofreaders: Annette Chartron, whose thorough attention to detail improved our prose, and Wendy Eidenmuller, whose unending patience with a steady stream of revisions made this final product possible. Finally, we thank our families for inspiring us, for being good sounding boards, and for tolerating for so long our obsession with this project.

Preface

This book is, written for the vocational student, whether studying a trade during high school or as an adult returning to school. It has been written because everyone we talk with about such education and training has agreed that these students will need more than technical skills to get a job, succeed at that job, and be promoted. They will need to be able to speak and listen effectively. Teachers know that; supervisors know that; future employers know that. Yet, present curricula probably do not include much direct instruction in oral communication.

This book, with its ideas and suggestions supported by testimony from successful vocational or technical graduates, supervisors, and employers, presents a brief background on the communication process and suggests the best ways to interact given the nature of that process. It is meant to be used as a supplement to English or Job-Related Training curricula and can be easily covered in its entirety in one nine-week period, or excerpts can be used here and there during any phase of the training program.

Throughout students' working lives, their abilities will be evaluated. Employers and supervisors will be asking routinely if a person *can* do a certain job, *will* do the job, and will *fit* in with others on the job. What one says and how it is said will enable them to answer those questions. The spoken word will be a catalyst for nearly all that one may accomplish both in work life and in personal life. Its mastery must not be taken for granted.

Contents

Oral Communication Skills

for Vo-Tech Students:
A Competency-Based Approach

PHOTOGRAPHY STUDIO help wanted . . . with people, telephone, and detail skills. . . .

MEDICAL OFFICE HELP wanted . . . professionalism and communication skills a must. . . .

I
Communication—
Who Needs It?

TECHNICIAN needed. . . . High school graduate with technical background, familiarity with laboratory environment, ability to communicate with various personnel. . . .

PIPE LAYER, Tractor backhoe operator . . . all applicants must be ambitious, outspoken. . . .

The Need for Communication throughout Society

Student Competency Goals

After reading this chapter, the student should be able to:

- Describe the steps involved in communicating ideas and feelings

- State how communication helps in one's personal life

- Explain how speaking and listening affect job success

Communication seems to be the "catch word" of this age. All manner of personal, business, scientific, and political problems are labeled "communication problems." Is this an appropriate label? What role does communication play in our personal and professional lives? And why does it seem to create so many problems?

The Communication Process Defined

To answer these questions, we must first understand the process being referred to as communication. Typically, communication includes two broad categories of activity: verbal and nonverbal — or with and without words. Verbal communication includes all sharing of ideas and feelings using words. Therefore, all that is *written* from prescriptions to newspapers to postcards to memos to operating manuals to novels is verbal communication. In addition, all *speaking* depends on verbal communication since we speak in words. But, our speaking also involves some non-word or nonverbal messages. Such nonverbal expression of ideas and feelings would include facial expressions, tone of voice, posture, gestures, the clothing we wear, and many other aspects of our actions that others see or hear.

Verbal and nonverbal messages are exchanged during the communication process. The process itself can best be explained by use of a model. Looking at the drawing below, we see that communication always involves at least two parties, each of whom acts as a sender/receiver. This two-part designation is appropriate because each of us sends verbal and nonverbal messages (speaks) at the same time that

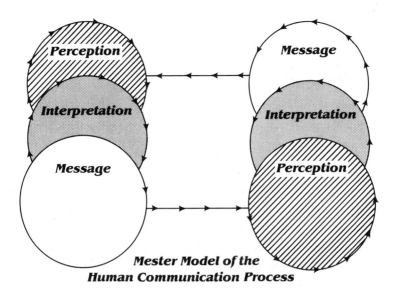

Mester Model of the Human Communication Process

we are receiving (hearing and seeing) nonverbal messages from our fellow communicator(s).

These two, or more, participants, then, can be thought of as simultaneously sharing verbal and nonverbal messages which are representations of their thoughts. The circles in the model reflect the continuous nature of communication. We are constantly involved in some interaction with others, and each interaction is affected by our previous interactions. We make and interpret messages in an ongoing cyclical manner.

The messages must pass through two separate transformations: first, from thought into words and/or gestures on the part of the first sender/receiver, and then from those words and/or gestures back into a thought in the mind of the second sender/receiver. In other words, first a thought is transformed by one person into some form that can be sent to others (the thought in its original form cannot be sent). That transmittable form might be a written word, a spoken word, a facial expression, or some artistic creation such as notes of music. The message in transmittable form is sent out through a medium such as a telephone, fax machine, or just through the air. The other person then receives that message in its verbal or nonverbal form and must transform it a second time, back into a thought —an interpretation in his/her own mind. Because of the message's transformations, there is enormous room for error.

The thought or understanding in the mind of the second person may not be exactly like the thought that originated in the mind of the first person. Misinterpretations occur because each person transforms the words, or facial expressions, or notes of music according to his/her own perspective. In the model, this phenomenon is represented by the filters through which messages pass as they are made and interpreted. For instance, you may think that the phrase "a few drops of oil" means six or eight drops, while I intended it to mean just two or three. If what we were talking about was peppermint oil for a frosting recipe, that difference in interpretation will spell the difference between a deliciously flavored frosting and one that tastes like toothpaste.

Given all of these factors, we can define comunication as the relatively imprecise process of exchanging verbal and nonverbal messages for the purpose of sharing ideas, information, and feelings.

The Need for Communication Skills

So, in all its imprecision, that is the communication process. Since the term communication refers to such a wide variety of everyday activities, it is a process that is central to most of what we do routinely. That is, regardless of our skills, we have a great deal of experience communicating. Communication is part of our relationships with friends and family. It is part of our lives as public citizens as we discuss and respond to political campaigns and controversies.

Just because we have experience as communicators does not necessarily mean that we are *skillful* as communicators. We have all had times in our experience as communicators in which we have become frustrated, been misunderstood, misunderstood others, or embarrassed ourselves. These communication errors have, perhaps, led to strained or broken relationships. For example, a friend may have asked to meet us at the corner of Sixth and State at 8:30 P.M. on Friday. We neglect to ask which part of that corner, and our friend hasn't clarified it in setting up the meeting. So, Friday at 8:30 P.M. our friend is waiting in the coffee shop on the northwest corner of Sixth and State, while we are waiting in the restaurant on the southeast corner. When the error is discovered, one of us is probably angry with the other. Why? All because of inadequate communication skill.

If we can be better speakers and listeners, we can derive more satisfaction from our personal lives and relationships. But, our personal lives are not the only arena in which we would benefit from improved communication.

Speaking and Your Job

We would not be able to accomplish much at all in our careers if we are unable to listen well, write clearly, or speak effectively. The connection between our job success and our communication skills is especially strong for spoken communication, both its verbal and nonverbal forms. There are many jobs in which one can be successful without having to do much writing in any form, but there are virtually no jobs in which one can succeed without speaking.

Let us examine that last statement more carefully by considering the following example of a typical workplace dialogue:

Jack Perkins has received a bill from Acme Auto Glass Company for a replacement windshield he ordered. Since he thought that he had already paid for the windshield, he stopped at the glass company on his way home from work. The secretary in the outer office greeted him and asked what he needed. Mr. Perkins explained the situation and asked her to check her records. She responded, "I'm not actually responsible for billing, but I could check with the bookkeeper for you tomorrow." Mr. Perkins answered, "Why tomorrow? Couldn't we check on it now since I'm here?" Just then Ms. Smith, the office manager, came out of an inner office, and the secretary called to her and explained Mr. Perkins's problem. Ms. Smith said she wasn't sure of the answer, but would check with Harry in the shop who had written up the work order. She called Harry to come check the bill. He looked it over and said, "There is some sort of mistake here because the windshield noted isn't the one we installed for Mr. Perkins." After further discussion, they all agreed that Mr. Perkins should not pay anything until the bookkeeper and the shop could doublecheck their records.

Now, answer the following questions about this example:

1. Could Ms. Smith have dealt with her customer in writing instead of by talking with him?

2. Would writing have been as effective as talking?

3. Was the talking actually necessary?

4. Was Ms. Smith's success affected by how well she said what she did?

5. What about Harry? Did he need to talk to do his job in this case?

6. What about the customer? Could he have done what he needed to do equally well by writing a letter instead of meeting with the glass company people?

7. Did the customer speak effectively enough?

8. Were any communication problems indicated in this example?

Your answers to the above questions should tell you that, indeed, comunication skills were quite relevant to the ability of all of these individuals to perform their tasks.

As we can see from the example, communication on the job often involves many different people. Since everybody has a different personality and different communication skills, each person's effectiveness in speaking and listening is different. It is sometimes a wonder that the communications work at all! But the most important point is that speaking and listening to one another is necessary to do a job. Whether the work involves talking someone into buying a used car, carrying on a conversation while giving someone a haircut, giving managers an oral report on your group's progress with a certain job, or telling a partner how high to hold the worklight, we all have to do some talking when working. How well one speaks can determine whether or not one keeps the job, gets a raise, or gets promoted. Do *you* realize how important oral communication is to *your* success?

Reference to Testimonials

For further discussion of the concepts and skills presented in this section, read the following paragraphs in the **Testimonials from the World of Work (IV):**

Testimonial 1. The Value of Oral Communication, Paragraphs 1.2-1.6, 1.13, and 1.14

Testimonial 2. The Importance of Oral Communication Skills in a Capstone Co-Op Program, Paragraphs 2.4 and 2.5

Testimonial 3. Importance of Telephone Skills in Customer Service, Paragraph 3.1

Testimonial 4. Oral Communication: A Roadblock to Student Success, Paragraphs 4.1, 4.4, and 4.6

Testimonial 5. Interpersonal Communication Skills, Paragraphs 5.1, 5.2, and 5.10

Testimonial 6. Communication: The Key to Advancement, Paragraphs 6.5 and 6.8

Testimonial 7. Making an Impression on the Telephone, Paragraph 7.1

Application Exercise

Objective: To demonstrate an appreciation of the role and importance of oral communication in all segments of our lives.

Activity: Select two situations where you could sit quietly and observe interactions between two people or among several people (such as, the library, the cafeteria, a service waiting area in a car dealership or repair shop, a bus stop, a store, or a doctor's office). For a 10- to 15-minute span in each situation, note the number of different oral communication interactions that occur and how many different people are involved. List the communication purposes that appear to have been served by each interaction.

The Need for Communcation Skills in the Workplace

Student Competency Goals

After reading this chapter, the student should be able to:

- Identify the DOT's three Worker Functions: *Data, People, Things*

- List the hierarchial skills within the category *People*

- Relate the category *People* to the proposition that all jobs require oral communication skills

- Describe the outcomes of need surveys which highlight the importance of oral communication skills

- Describe the results of literature reviews which highlight the importance of oral communication skills

- Defend the need for oral communication skills in vo-tech trades

Few people could successfully dispute the need for oral communication skills in our day-to-day existence. Whether ordering a pizza, making a concert reservation, talking with a friend, discussing a movie, or simply asking directions, oral communication skills are essential. Oral communication skills are no less important in the world of work.

Dictionary of Occupational Titles

Who says vocational-technical school graduates will have to orally communicate when they enter the world of work? Among others, the United States Department of Labor's 1977 *Dictionary of Occupational Titles* (DOT) says so. This document contains over 30,000 concise definitions for occupational titles common to today's workplace, especially those representing vo-tech careers. The DOT structures and analyzes the total world of work, paying special attention to defining specific worker skills and actions.

According to the DOT, *every job* demands that workers function effectively with the categories *Data, People,* and *Things.* These categories help analyze exactly what a worker does on each job. Although a worker's job may vary with regard to these categories, *no job escapes at least some responsibility* within each category.

The category *Data* involves a range of skills and responsibilities, from Comparing and Copying to Coordinating and Synthesizing. It involves the use of numbers, fractions, symbols, measurements, and ratios. Examples would be using ratios to mix chemicals in cosmetology or to create the correct "mix" for working concrete on a scorching hot day.

Things, as a second category of Worker Functions, involves manipulation of materials, machines, tools, equipment, and products, from Handling and Tending materials to Precision Working and Set Up of equipment. Operating equipment such as a turret lathe in machine shop, a radial arm saw in carpentry, or a 35-mm camera in Commercial Arts is all included.

The category *People,* the third set of Worker Functions and the one of the most concern in this book, involves relationships with other individuals such as Taking Instructions, Serving, Negotiating, and Mentoring. Most often these relationships involve oral communication. Whether one is talking with fellow workers, asking clarifying questions, training others, or interacting with customers, communication is a necessary worker function. Plainly and simply, one cannot exist, let alone advance, in today's work world without effective communication skills.

A complete list of the DOT's *People* communication skills is shown below. Each skill is numbered, and the *lower* the number, the *more* challenging the worker responsibility.

Skills within the *People* Category

0—Mentoring: Dealing with individuals in terms of their total personality in order to advise, counsel, and/or guide them with regard to problems that may be resolved by legal, scientific, clinical, spiritual, and/or other professional principles

1—Negotiating: Exchanging ideas, information, and opinions with others to formulate policies and programs and/or arrive jointly at decisions, conclusions, or solutions

2—Instructing: Teaching subject matter to others; or training others through explanation, demonstration, and supervised practice; or making recommendations on the basis of technical disciplines

3—Supervising: Determining or interpreting work procedures for a group of workers, assigning specific duties to them, maintaining harmonious relations among them, and promoting efficiency

4—Diverting: Amusing others (stage, screen, radio, television)

5—Persuading: Influencing others in favor of a product, service, or point of view

6—Speaking-Signaling: Talking with and/or signaling people to convey or exchange information, including giving assignments and/or directions to helpers or assistants

7—Serving: Attending to the needs or requests of people or to the expressed or implicit wishes of people; immediate response is involved

8—**Taking Instructions-Helping:** Helping applies to "non-learning" helpers; no variety of responsibility involved

Take a moment and think how the *People* category — the world of oral communication — applies to *your* trade. Would it be possible to advance in *your* trade without possessing effective communication skills? For that matter, would it be possible even to continue in *your* trade without such skills?

Who says oral communication skills apply to vo-tech careers? Not just academic and vocational teachers, nor just those already working in a chosen field. The *Dictionary of Occupational Titles* says so — loud and clear! Without a doubt, the *People* functions and skills verify that *every known occupation* involves some form of oral communication.

Employers and Educators Speak Out

A survey by the authors further reinforces the perceived importance of oral communication skills. We surveyed those most directly involved with vocational-technical preparation at an area vocational-technical school (AVTS): the AVTS shop instructors, employers, Craft Advisory Committee members, and seniors taking part in co-op work experiences. This AVTS serves students from ten school districts on a "week-about" system, that is, one week at the home academic school and one week at the AVTS. Sixteen labs, from cosmetology and food service to tool and die and electronics technology, are offered. Approximately 630 sophomores, juniors, and seniors participate in the program each year.

Interview-type surveys, completed in person or over the phone, were used. The respondents were first provided with a brief explanation of the Data, People, and Things categories as described in the DOT. Then, the respondents were asked to rate the relative importance of these three categories of DOT worker-functions to a vo-tech graduate's success.

All those surveyed indicated the People category to be *more important* than the Data category and *as important* as the Things category. Whether they were vo-tech instructors, employers, Craft Advisory Committee members, or vo-tech students participating in co-op experiences, *all* respondents ranked the People category (oral communicaiton) as high or higher than the other two categories. These people should know what they are talking about!

A related survey conducted at the same time by a nearby comprehensive vocational-technical high school's General Advisory Committee again confirmed the importance of oral communcation skills. Their survey presented over 1,100 participants with fourteen educational concerns and/or personality traits and asked them to rank the importance of the traits in connection with the hiring of vo-tech graduates. The following table summarizes this survey's results, with "1" representing the *highest* ranking position.

Erie City Tech Survey: Summary Results of the Vocational Education Curriculum Enhancement Survey			
	Business Rank	Educators Rank	Students Rank
Attendance/Dependability	1	1	1
Positive Attitude	2	2	3
Oral Communication	3	3	5
Problem Solving/Reasoning	4	4	8
Self-Confidence*	5	5	2
Interpersonal Relationships	6	10/11	11
Personal Appearance	7	9	7
Flexibility	8	12	10
Safety Awareness	9	7	4
Technical Skills	10	6	6
Written Communication	11	8	12
Mathematical Skills	12	10/11	9
Understanding of Free Enterprise System	13	14	13
Familiarity with Computers	14	13	14
*Self-Confidence and Oral Communication are correlated.			

Three different audiences (employers, educators, and vo-tech students), independently surveyed, all arrived at the same conclusion: oral communication is ranked among the top characteristics influencing the hiring of vo-tech graduates. Businessmen/women and educators ranked oral communication No. 3, while students ranked it No. 5. As for the students who ranked Self-Confidence No. 2, it should be pointed out that Self-Confidence is most readily displayed in the form of oral communication.

Surprising as it may seem, Oral Communication was ranked well above Technical Skills by *all* participants. What this means is, given a choice, participants would hire someone who possesses technical skills in the trade *and* oral communication skills before they would hire someone who just possesses technical skills in the trade.

Further, Oral Communication was ranked well above Mathematical Skills among hiring considerations. Given the relative importance shown for these two skills, it is somewhat ironic that most vo-tech schools formally teach job-related mathematics, but, as yet, do not formally teach job-related oral communication skills.

Vocational-Technical Research

"All other things being equal, it is not the superior skill in the processes of the occupation which will determine an individual's advancement; it is the superior skill in oral communication." With these words in 1954, William Hawley identified the key basic skills needed by all high school graduates. In the years since, numerous researchers have observed that training students in oral communication is a very important part of preparing them for the world of work, whether at the entry level or for advancement.

Research in the field of vocational-technical school programs clearly has concluded that basic-skills instruction is as critical to the students' job success as technical trade instruction. Although employers remain interested in hiring people who have received occupationally specific training, they also want individuals with a solid grounding in basic skills ("Employers' Expectations of Vocational Education," 1990). Within the broad area of basic skills, oral communication is ranked highly as a factor in job success. Carnevale,

Gainer, Meltzer (1989) stress that job-related skills go beyond mere reading and writing. Among the seven "skills employers want," oral communication and listening were third most important. Rosenfeld (1988) reinforces the importance of communication skills, both speaking and listening, in the preparation of youth and adults for employment.

In a summary report produced by the Illinois State Board of Education (Greenan, 1983), employers rated the "generalizable skills" across all vocational education curricula in the state. The single skill considered most generalizable (most important in all trades) was "interpersonal relations." Interpersonal relations is defined as using oral communication to work with peers and to interact with superiors.

The vocational-technical students' need for listening skills, an important part of the oral communication process, is quite prominent in the literature. Respondents in a survey of technical school graduates ranked "effective listening" as the number-one communication skill they actually used on the job (Pointer, 1985).

The value of oral communication instruction is further stressed in the literature of educational philosophy. Ernest Boyer (1983), past United States Secretary of Education, emphasized the need to upgrade the basic skills in technical school curricula. He cited a survey of American business in which over half of the respondents indicated that the high school graduates they hired had serious problems with speaking and listening effectively. Many who philosophize what ought to be in a high school curriculum concur with the empirical researchers that there is an observable relationship between oral communication skills and job success for the vocational-technical school graduate.

Reference to Testimonials

For further discussion of the concepts and skills presented in this section, read the following paragraphs in the **Testimonials from the World of Work** (IV):

Testimonial 1. The Value of Oral Communcation, Paragraphs 1.2-1.5, 1.9, and 1.14

Testimonial 2. The Importance of Oral Communication Skills in a Capstone Co-Op Program, Paragraphs 2.3-2.5 and 2.8

Testimonial 4. Oral Communication: A Roadblock to Student Success, Paragraphs 4.1, 4.2, and 4.4

Testimonial 9. Making an Impression on the Telephone, Paragraph 9.1

Testimonial 11. Society and Communication, Paragraphs 11.1, 11.2, 11.4, 11.6, 11.7, and 11.8

Testimonial 12. Communication Means Success or Failure in Construction, Paragraph 12.1

Testimonial 14. "Didn't You Hear What I Said?", Paragraph 14.1

Application Exercises

Objective: To verify the importance of oral communication skills to vo-tech graduates' job success.

Activity: Interview, in person or over the telephone, local employers in your trade to determine the importance of oral communication. Inquire as to how important oral communication skills are to, first, getting the job and, second, advancing within the company. Discuss your findings with other class members.

Objective: To apply the DOT's *People* category to one's career area.

Activity: On an individual basis, identify how the skills within the DOT's *People* category apply to your career area. Meet with other students in the same career area, share results, and arrive at a consensus. Meet with students in other career areas, and take turns explaining how the *People* category applies to each career area.

References

Boyer, E.L., *High School: A Report on Secondary Education in America*, New York: Harper and Row, 1983.

Carnevale, A. P., Gainer, L.J., and Meltzer, A.S., *Work-place Bas-*

ics: The Skills Employers Want. Alexandria, VA: American Society for Training and Development (ERIC Document, Accession No. 299 462), 1989.

"Employers' Expectations of Vocational Education," ERIC *Digest No. 90*, Columbus, OH: Center on Education and Training for Employment, The Ohio State University, 1990.

Greenan, J.P., *Identification of Generalizable Skills in Secondary Vocational Programs*, Springfield, IL: Illinois State Board of Education, 1983.

Hawley, W.B., "Speech Plays Its Part in Occupational Success," *NASSP Bulletin, 38*:133, 1954.

Painter, C.M., "A Survey of Communication Skills Needed On-the-Job by Technical Students," *Journal of Studies in Technical Careers, 7*:3, 1985.

Rosenfeld, S.A., "Educating for the Factories of the Future," *Education Week*, June 22, 1988.

United States Department of Labor, *Dictionary of Occupational Titles*, Washington, D.C., 1977.

MEDICAL ASSISTANT for . . . . Experience preferred, good interpersonal skills required.

COMPUTER PROGRAMMER . . . two to three years experience . . . good interpersonal skills. . . .

II
Interpersonal Communication Skills for Work

MECHANIC III . . . one year of vocational training or . . . be able to follow written and oral instructions. . . .

AUTO PARTS TRAINEES . . . . Openings for energetic, mechanically oriented individuals with good interpersonal communication. . . .

Talking to Get the Job: The Interview

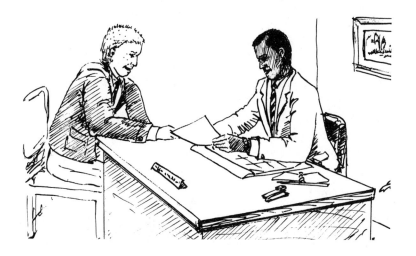

Student Competency Goals

After reading this chapter, the student should be able to:

- Anticipate the questions that may be asked in a job interview

- Understand the importance of looking for relationships that connect the questions asked

- Formulate clear, relevant answers to interview questions

- Phrase intelligent questions to ask during interviews

- Dress appropriately for job interviews

In order to be hired, no matter what your job skills, you must have certain speaking and listening skills. In most trades, there are more qualified applicants than there are openings. So, how does the employer choose among the applicants?

Employers want to know three basic things about any applicant: Can he/she do the job (have the necessary job skills)? Will he/she do the job (motivated to work)? Will he/she fit in at this job? The first question may be answered by looking at the applicant's written application. But the other two can *only* be answered by interviewing the applicant and drawing conclusions about the person's motivation, character, and style from the way the individual communicates during the interview.

Projecting a Positive Image

The old saying, "It's not what you know, but who you know," is often true. But it is not the *only* way applicants are selected. Another valid interpretation of that old saying is that the "who" referred to could be yourself. In other words, the job applicant who speaks knowledgeably and assertively about him/herself has a definite edge over the applicant whose manner reflects a lack of self-confidence. Let us examine the following examples:

Interview No. 1

Mr. Smith: "Good morning, Joe. I see you are interested in the job we have available in our typesetting room."

Joe: "Yes, sir."

Mr. Smith: "Tell me about your experience."

Joe: "Well, I graduated from the graphics program at vo-tech and worked part-time at my uncle's print shop."

Interview No. 2

Mr. Smith: "Good morning, Marge. I see you are interested in the job we have available in our typesetting room."

Marge: "Yes, sir. I have been working for a year in a small print shop, and I think it's time for me to move on to a more diversified company."

Mr. Smith: "I see — well, tell me about your experience."

Marge: "I graduated a year ago from the graphics program at vo-tech. During that time, I worked part-time and did my co-op experience at the small print shop I mentioned. After graduation, I was hired to work more hours, though still part time. My responsibilities there have basically been limited to the poster business."

These two interviews are off to very different starts. In the first case, Joe has given the interviewer only a minimum of information about himself and has not taken advantage of this early opportunity to create a positive first impression about his own professionalism. On the other hand, Marge has given the interviewer several specific details about herself and has done so in a way that conveys her self-confidence and professional approach to the job situation. Assuming that the two interviews were to continue along these contrasting lines, it is likely that Marge would be offered the job over Joe, even though their actual backgrounds and experiences are quite similar.

The job interview, then, is the first hurdle to be crossed in using communication skills effectively for a job. The particular skills the applicant should demonstrate during the interview are listening, phrasing of answers and questions, oral grammar, and nonverbal appearance.

Listening

Did you know that we spend about twice as much of our time listening as we do using any other communication skill? Yet very little time is spent actually learning *how* to listen well.

Listening effectively involves two important skills. The first is being *mentally* attentive. That is, you must focus your mind on the speaker and his/her point. It is very easy to be distracted by items you see in the room, by noises you hear, or even by one word or idea mentioned in passing by the speaker. But you must not give in to those distractions, and instead must have "tunnel hearing."

Before going into the interview, you should remind yourself what the purpose of the interview is and what information the interviewer will most likely try to get from you. By making mental notes ahead of time, you will be helping to focus your attention. The interviewer is probably going to ask questions about:

1. Your educational background

2. Your training and experience in the trade

3. Your previous jobs

4. Your career goals

You should have these items in mind as the interviewer asks questions. By doing so, you are more likely to correctly interpret the question's purpose, no matter how it may be phrased.

Besides being mentally attentive as a listener in an interview, you must be *physically* attentive. In other words, your body language ought to convey an interest in the speaker's words. An interviewee should look comfortable and natural as long as "natural" is not sloppy and lazy. Sit upright in the chair with both feet firmly on the floor or crossed at the ankles. Try to sit reasonably still while listening so that you do not appear unduly nervous—without squirming or fidgeting when the interviewer speaks.

As the interviewer is asking questions, you should be looking him/her in the eyes. Such direct eye contact will be interpreted as a sign of sincerity, self-confidence, and interest.

By exhibiting such mental and physical attentiveness, you, the interviewee, will create a comfortable and positive atmosphere for the interview as you begin to answer questions.

Speaking: Questions and Answers

All answers to interview questions should be carefully — and quickly — thought out. Remember that your purpose is both to provide information and to create a positive image of yourself as a person. One without the other is not enough. Looking back to our examples at the start of an interview, we can see several differences in the way answers were stated:

> In responding concerning his interest in this opening, Joe simply established that he was interested. Marge, however, established *why* she was interested in the job (looking for a more diversified company).

So the first important point to make about answers is that they are opportunities to clarify and expand upon your qualifications for the position sought. Without overdoing it, it is appropriate to elaborate somewhat, rather than answering with a simple yes or no. Remember that the interviewer has reviewed your *written* application. What he/she needs to hear in the *oral* interview is background or reasoning behind the written answers.

> In referring to the previous work experience, Joe stated that he had worked in his uncle's print shop; however, Marge stated that she had worked in a small print shop.

Even though the circumstances of the job might have been the same for both applicants, Marge's phrasing was better. Why? Joe referred to the shop as his uncle's, suggesting he might have gotten the job because of his family relationship. Marge's answer, on the other hand, contained no such implication. Her answer did not put a negative slant on her background qualifications, while Joe's answer did. Your answers to all questions should provide the requested information in a way that makes you look as good as possible. Again, remember that your answers should provide information and enhance your image.

> In describing his previous work experience, Joe simply said he worked at the print shop; Marge described how long she had worked there and the work she had done.

Marge's answer was preferable because it provided relatively specific information on her previous responsibilities, giving the interviewer a clearer sense of her actual skills than Joe did. In addition, by elaborating a little, Marge capitalized on the opportunity to demonstrate her oral communication skills. Since oral communication skills are related to job success, the interviewer needs to evaluate them. Marge gave the interviewer that opportunity to evaluate; Joe did not. Answers, then, should be complete, providing reasonable detail about the issue raised in the interviewer's question, and doing so in as articulate a manner as possible.

Skillful answering of questions in an interview can be achieved by keeping several guidelines in mind. First, remember that each of your answers should provide the requested information clearly and completely. Second, remember that each answer should help establish a positive image of your background, talents, and character. Finally, remember that both of these objectives should be accomplished in a way that permits you to demonstrate reasonably good oral communication skills.

Oral Grammar

The last point brings us to an issue that deserves special consideration as you prepare for the job interview: oral grammar. We have all painstakingly studied grammar in our language's written form. Too often, though, we fail to transfer those principles to our oral language. Instead, we allow colloquialisms that we would never think of using in writing to become commonplace in speaking.

Naturally, there are some colloquial expressions that are acceptable in speaking because they are still grammatically correct. For instance, "okay" is considered to be appropriate in spoken English. But there are many other language habits that are totally unacceptable. Anyone seeking to impress an interviewer should therefore be cautious in their use. The most frequent offenders are:

1. Double negatives: "I didn't do no ordering."
2. Noun-verb disagreement: "My boss don't need to supervise me."
3. Ain't: "I ain't ever worked on a turret lathe."
4. Like: "Like, my boss never, like, keeps track of my, like, hours."
5. Y'know: "I think, y'know, that this move would be good for me."

See the Application Exercises at the end of this chapter if you need work on avoiding double negatives or noun-verb disagreements. In addition, you can work to eliminate the presence of any of the five habitual errors in your oral grammar by using a tape recorder. Tape record one of your casual conversations with a friend, then listen to it to determine if you seem habitually to misuse "ain't," "like," or "y'know." If you do, concentrate on avoiding them in casual conversation.

Once you limit their use in your casual language, it is unlikely that you will use them in the more formal setting of a job interview. Correct oral grammar is one way to enhance your image as an intelligent, attentive person in the interview, and to increase your chances of being hired.

Personal Appearance

In addition to being a good listener and answering questions well, your success in the job interview will be influenced by the nonverbal factor, your physical appearance. Your appearance helps the interviewer to form some influential first impressions about your character. By appearance, we are not talking about your natural beauty or your height or weight — these are factors over which you have relatively little control. The interviewer will judge your appearance in regard to what you *do* with those "givens."

"Clean" and "neat" ought to be your guidewords when preparing for an interview. Therefore, you need to give yourself enough time to shower, shave, do your hair, and select an appropriate outfit. Men should wear well-fitting, clean, pressed slacks and shirt or sweater (though a sport coat may be appropriate for some jobs).

The style of clothing should be relatively plain so that your appearance does not distract from your words. The same principle holds true for your hair, which should be recently cut and styled. For women, well-fitting, clean, pressed slacks or skirt worn with a blouse or sweater would be appropriate. If a skirt is selected, the hemline should be below the knee. Any jewelry, like the outfit itself, should be modest and nondistracting. Your hair style and makeup should also be moderate.

Your physical appearance will be one factor on which the interviewer bases some assumptions about your reliability, maturity, and responsibility as a worker. Therefore, you should make conscious and careful decisions about your appearance just as you do about your verbal messages.

In the job interview, you have a golden opportunity to emphasize your job skills and professionalism as a potential employee. You will take advantage of that opportunity best by using good communication skills. Your verbal and nonverbal strategies are tools that will help you to get the desired job, and to establish a good first impression that will be an asset as you work for advancement.

Reference to Testimonials

For further discussion of the concepts and skills presented in this section, read the following paragraphs in the **Testimonials from the World of Work (IV):**

Testimonial 1. The Value of Oral Communication, Paragraph 1.9

Testimonial 2. The Importance of Oral Communication Skills in a Capstone Co-Op Program, Paragraph 2.4

Testimonial 4. Oral Communication: A Roadblock to Student Success, Paragraph 4.2

Testimonial 5. Interpersonal Communication Skills, Paragraph 5.1

Testimonial 10. Communicating in the Solitary World of Masonry, Paragraphs 10.2-10.7

Application Exercises

Objective: To demonstrate understanding of questions to be anticipated in a job interview, the best ways to answer them, and questions that might be asked by the interviewee.

Activities: First, list three general questions that may be asked in a job interview to assess a candidate's character. With a partner, talk about how those questions could best be answered to establish your trustworthiness, dependability, and dedication as an employee.

List three specific questions that may be asked about your personal work experience. With a partner, talk about how those questions could best be answered to establish your trade skills and achievements.

List three questions you would like to ask interviewers about the job situations for which you might apply.

Finally, role-play interviews using the above nine questions in front of the class.

Objective: To recognize and correct obvious grammatical errors in conversational speaking.

Activity: There are 14 errors in the following conversation. The errors include double negatives, noun-verb disagreements, and the wrong form of pronouns. Circle each error and indicate the type of error by writing DN, NVD, or WFP above your circle. Then rewrite the conversation correcting each error:

Joe: "Good morning, Mary. I seen you at the PTA meeting last night. What did you think of it?"

Mary: "Morning, Joe. Well, I'll tell you, them officers are in for a long year if the parents aren't no more cooperative than they was last night. Nobody wants to help out at the school."

Joe: "That's right. Nobody never raised their hands when they asked for help even on little things like stuffing envelopes."

Mary: "You and me and the Joneses was the only ones who worked on building the playground. We just can't do everything! I'm not going to stop helping, but I'm not going to do it alone neither."

Joe: "What can we do? The president done everything except get down on her knees to beg people to help. It don't seem to make no difference."

Mary: "Let's ask Hazel next time we see her how they do it at her kids' school. She's always talking about what a good thing they have at PTA."

Joe: "That's the truth. She and them kids are always working on some project over there."

Mary: "She's even went on field trips with them. Well, we better punch in. We don't want nobody saying we're socializing on company time."

Talking on the Job: You and Your Supervisor

Student Competency Goals

After reading this chapter, the student should be able to:

- Interpret supervisor instructions accurately

- Understand the best ways to question a supervisor

- Communicate respect for oneself and supervisor nonverbally

Now that your communication skills have helped you to get a job you know you are qualified for, it's time to proceed with polishing those skills in order to keep the job and to succeed in it. You will be communicating with a wide variety of people in any job situation. The three broad groups of people with whom you must speak clearly and purposefully are your supervisors, your customers or clients, and your coworkers. Each of the three groups requires specific communication skills as well as a range of general communication skills.

We shall begin with the very important use of effective oral communication in interactions with your supervisors. As in any communication setting, your success will in part depend on having the proper attitude as you approach the interaction. That proper attitude includes a healthy respect for the possibility of error in any communication and a commitment to work cooperatively to minimize any such error and its potential impact. As we polish our communication skills, we must continually realize that no matter how careful we are in creating and interpreting messages, there will always be room for error.

Listening: Following Directions

Remember that being an effective oral communicator involves both speaking and listening. Listening to your supervisors, especially early in your career, means listening to oral directions more often than to anything else. Do you follow directions well? If you do, or if you believe you can do better, your skill probably stems from your ability to perceive the connections among the many details given to you in directions. Consider what would be going through your mind if you were listening to the following directions:

> You are going to be working today on framing the left-end walls for these housing units. For each one, you will need eight 2×4s set on 16-inch centers, secured top and bottom with number 12 nails, and with alternating spanners approximately 3-1/2 feet from top or bottom.

These directions are fairly simple and clear, yet could easily be misinterpreted if you allow yourself to get caught up in the details. In other words, listening and making mental notes of just the details —eight 2×4s, 16-inch centers, number 12s, 3-1/2-foot spanners — could cause you to lose the overall sense of what to do with those details — build a wall.

The best way to listen to directions is to attempt to grasp the overall picture. As the supervisor begins speaking, listen to understand the basic job you are being asked to do. Then, as each detail is stated, you can understand it in relation to that overall assignment, and, thus, more clearly remember the details.

You will understand better how to do something when you understand its function within an overall task. It is a serious listening mistake to try to absorb that series of details as a list of separate entities. You are trying to remember six or eight separate, meaningful pieces of information instead of one broad piece with six or eight related "bytes" of information. The human mind is much better suited to the latter way of functioning, and, therefore, that is the way you should listen.

A second suggestion for better listening when supervisors are giving directions is to avoid being distracted. Just as concentration and focus were necessary when listening during the interview, they are necessary when listening to instructions. Tune your ears "into" the supervisor's voice. Focus on the words and the vocal expression accompanying them, excluding everything else happening around you. That might be difficult if you are in a noisy shop or a place where many other conversations are going on, but it is vital.

By focusing on the specific information you are supposed to be listening to, you will decrease your chances of wandering off on a mental tangent, and will increase your understanding significantly. If you allow yourself to wonder what that guy is doing at the next table or whether you might be able to get a date with that certain someone speaking in the background, you will not even *hear* your supervisor's instructions, let alone *understand* them.

A third and final suggestion for listening to your supervisor has to do with expecting clarity. Just becasue a person is a supervisor does not necessarily mean that he/she is good at giving directions. A supervisor is as likely as anyone else to make an error in phrasing a message, and, as a listener, you must be alert to that possibility. This does not mean that you ought to be listening defensively, ready to find fault with what the supervisor says, which is always counterproductive. Rather, it means to listen intelligently. If a particular word or phrase is unclear to you, ask about it. It may be that the speaker made an unconscious slip, or that a wrong word was used, or that you don't have the background to understand what was said.

Whatever the cause, the speaker cannot correct your confusion unless you communicate it. So, don't be afraid to interrupt to ask intelligent questions. Furthermore, because an error unrecognized by either of you is possible, it is always wise to repeat directions you have been given briefly before leaving the supervisor. That is the best way to find out quickly if the supervisor has given an incorrect instruction, or if you have misunderstood something. Better to clarify the error before building walls with sixteen 2×4s instead of eight!

Requesting Information

That brings us to another situation in which you will need to communicate effectively with your supervisor: asking questions. You will need to ask many questions about your work, your schedule, and your responsibilities. The way you phrase those questions, your manner of approaching the supervisor, and even the timing of your questions can contribute to the supervisor's perception of your value as an employee.

Every time you need to ask a question, remember that it should be carefully planned to get the information you need most clearly and efficiently, while presenting yourself to the supervisor in the best possible light. In other words, you want to look good to the supervisor during this communication opportunity. The careful planning called for need only take a few seconds if you are just asking an easy question about a task. However, it may take several days of thinking to plan how best to ask for something sensitive such as extra vacation time.

Your planning should begin by mentally clarifying what it is you need to know, as specifically as possible. For instance, in doing an auto repair estimate, you may be unclear about how much work the customer wants done. Establish clearly in your own mind whether you don't understand the whole order or just a specific part of the order such as the amount of repainting desired. By narrowing the focus of your question, you will get a more useful answer from the supervisor; you will use the supervisor's time more efficiently; and you will represent yourself as a clear thinker.

Once you have done this clarification, you are ready to plan the actual phrasing of the question. Always use the most specific, technically appropriate terms when speaking with a supervisor. Asking about a "thingamajig" will make it difficult for the supervisor to understand you, causing him/her to think less of your technical abilities than you might like. In addition, your question should be phrased to show appropriate respect for the supervisor, for his/her expertise and authority. Use proper grammar, avoid colloquialisms, and address the supervisor as "sir," or "ma'am," or by first name if appropriate in the particular situation.

With these two planning steps accomplished, you are ready to actually ask your question. Pick the right time. One personnel director tells the story of employee named Tom who, while working on his lathe, stopped his supervisor to ask about repairing the shower in the employee locker room. The supervisor responded angrily; Tom filed a grievance with the union; and the whole problem mushroomed, taking valuable time from several people over a two-week period. Had Tom picked a better time to ask the question, when his work would not have been interrupted and his supervisor was not rushed, the whole matter could have been resolved much more smoothly.

Naturally, if your question is about a task you are working on at the time, that question will need to be asked almost immediately, and you shouldn't waste work time by waiting to ask it. However, there are some questions that are not of immediate impact, and, therefore, you can choose when to ask them. These might include questions about the supervisor's evaluation of your work, questions about working conditions, or personal questions. For these you will get a fuller, more satisfying answer if you ask at a time when the supervisor is relatively unrushed and in a good mood.

Every person operates differently, some being at their best early in the morning and others being more relaxed and easy to talk with later in the day. If you need to ask a favor of your supervisor, try to be sensitive to that best time of day for him/her.

To review, asking questions of your supervisor is a necessary communication task in which you can simultaneously get needed information and enhance the supervisor's perception of you as a worker. To accomplish both goals, your questions should be carefully planned by being focused and well phrased, and should be asked at the best possible time.

Establishing Mutual Respect

If you are a good listener when supervisors are giving directions, and your own questions of the supervisor are effective, then you have laid the communication groundwork for establishing mutual respect between yourself and your supervisor. Such mutual respect is extremely important to your job success and advancement. In all you say and do in interactions with your supervisor, you want to show a sincere interest in performing well on the job and professionalism in your approach.

You will communicate such a positive attitude by both verbal and nonverbal behavior. The supervisor needs to trust your judgment and respect your workmanship. You can encourage this response by the same communication strategies that were described as important to the interview.

Specifically, in all interactions with a supervisor, establish direct eye contact. This shows interest and commitment to clear communication, and provides a good opprotunity for useful feedback during the conversation. By looking directly at the supervisor, you communicate respect for that person and trust in your own abilities to interact effectively with him/her.

Secondly, be clear and complete in all your communication. This shows a respect for demands on the supervisor's time, and it reflects an intelligent approach to the difficulties of effective communication. Such clarity is achieved by careful word choice and appropriate accompanying nonverbal messages. The supervisor does not have time for anyone to "beat around the bush" when there are jobs to be done, and your recognition of that constraint will be appreciated.

Finally, you can establish respect for your supervisor and for your job by your appearance. A neat appearance on the job, as well as a record of promptness, shows that you have a professional attitude deserving of the supervisor's attention. The little things the supervisor notices about you as you do your work are important to his/her developing appraisal of your skills and attitudes.

Communicating effectively with a supervisor is one of the most important elements of any job. The supervisor will frequently give oral directions and expect you to be an attentive listener. There will also be occasions when you need to ask the supervisor a question, or just talk about your work. As both a listener and speaker, you have the opportunity to demonstrate communication skills while learning what you need to know to do your job correctly. You can capitalize on such opportunities by listening for overall concepts, listening with concentration, planning questions carefully, asking intelligent questions, and speaking with respect for yourself, your work, and your supervisor.

Reference to Testimonials

For further discussion of the concepts and skills presented in this section, read the following paragraphs in the **Testimonials from the World of Work (IV):**

Testimonial 1. The Value of Oral Communication, Paragraphs 1.5 and 1.10

Testimonial 5. Interpersonal Communication Skills, Paragraphs 5.3, 5.5, 5.6, and 5.9

Testimonial 6. Communication: The Key to Advancement, Paragraphs 6.2 and 6.5

Testimonial 10. Communicating in the Solitary World of Masonry, Paragraphs 10.8, 10.9, and 10.11

Testimonial 12. Communication Means Success or Failure in Construction, Paragraphs 12.1, 12.2, 12.5-12.7

Testimonial 13. Facing the Challenge of Communication, Paragraphs 13.2 and 13.4

Testimonial 14. "Didn't You Kear What I Said?", Paragraphs 14.2 and 14.5

Application Exercise

Objective: To demonstrate understanding of the principle of listening for main ideas, and distinguishing between what is important and what is extraneous to spoken messages.

Activity: Listen to the operating instructions your teacher will read to you. They will be read just once, so pay close attention. Now write what you think were the four main points in that set of instructions. Compare your responses with the points highlighted in the written instructions the teacher will show.

Talking on the Job: You and the Customer

Student Competency Goals

After reading this chapter, the student should be able to:

- Identify situations on the job when it would be necessary to talk with a client or customer one-to-one

- Ask clear questions of clients that convey interest in the answers

- Engage the client in pleasant, supportive social conversation

- Speak comprehensibly and courteously on the telephone

- Plan and present effective, persuasive interpersonal messages for a particular client

Many of you reading this book are studying for a vocation in which you will provide a service to the public, a client or customer.

Consequently, there will be many times when you must speak on a one-to-one basis to the person for whom you are providing the service.

One-to-one interactions with the public are not reserved solely for "front-office" personnel or supervisors. Any employee may need communication skills in this type of interaction. For convience, this chapter will use the term "client" to refer to any member of the public for whom a service is provided, whether that person may be more appropriately labelled "customer," "patient," "guest," etc. Skill in interpersonal communication with clients will contribute significantly to career success and advancement.

Questions for the Client

A large proportion of your interpersonal communication with clients will center on asking and answering questions. The cosmetologist may ask what type of a haircut the client wants. The restaurant host/hostess may ask where the client would prefer to sit. The metal fabricator may ask about the precise specifications a client wants a product to meet. The carpenter may ask how many shelves the client wants in the closet being built. The health care worker may ask about the client's degree of comfort. These are only a few examples of the thousands of questions that may come up in ordinary work routines.

Regardless of the specific subject matter, your questions need to be well phrased. Your meaning should be clear and your motivation for asking should appear nonbiased. These general guidelines can be met by following a few specific principles to help achieve the goals of any work-related questions: getting clear information and establishing a positive relationship.

First, choose the most precise terms appropriate for the client, who is typically not an expert in your field. In your education, you have learned a range of very clear trade terms that facilitate your interaction with your coworkers and supervisors on the job. Remember, your clients have not learned those terms. If you work in commercial foods, you know very well the differences between the grades of beef as defined by the U.S. Department of Agriculture. But, since your clients don't, it serves no purpose for you to ask if they prefer a "prime" or "choice" cut. Instead, you might show them examples of the various grades of beef you have available and ask which they prefer.

In interpreting the client's answers to your questions, you must be equally cautious about your understanding of trade terms. The classic barbershop request to "take a little off the top" can be interpreted dozens of ways. You had better find out what the client means before you start cutting! Asking, "Would you like me to cut about half an inch, or more like a quarter of an inch?" may seem terribly imprecise to you as a professional. But to the client who cannot visualize five-sixteenths of an inch of anything, it is a better question than one using the precise measurements you learned in cosmetology.

Secondly, in addition to avoiding trade terms, your phrasing of questions should adhere to guidelines of objectivity. That is, you should not ask biased or leading questions. An example of such a question from a mechanic sent out to rescue a stranded motorist might be, "You didn't try to jump start this yourself, did you?" This is considered to be a leading question because the expected answer is implied by the phrasing of the question. It is also a biased question because it implies that if you did try to jump start the car, you shouldn't have. Thus, your question will likely both fail to get a clear answer (the client being unsure whether to tell the truth) and insult the client's intelligence—resulting in a double death knell to effective interaction. A better question would have been the more straightforward, "Did you try to jump-start the car?"

A third prinicple to follow regarding the phrasing of questions is that they should be phrased in a positive rather than negative way. A negative question such as, "If you don't mind, will you please sign right here?" invites confusion. Answering "yes" to the question could be the client's way of saying, "Yes, I do mind; so I won't sign." Or the client could just as easily mean, "Yes, I'll sign." Even a "no" to this question is less than totally clear. Don't make a client try to guess what you mean.

Even though your questions may be well phrased, they still could be misunderstood; so, you should always feel comfortable about asking follow-up questions. These can help to clarify both your thinking and that of the client. In a restaurant setting, for instance, you may ask if a client would prefer a table or a booth. Your question seems fairly clear, but the client may not fully realize that his/her answer will be the only factor used to select the dining spot. He/she might say, "Anywhere is fine," when, in truth, a table not too close to the kitchen and away from the salad table is preferred. It would be wise in this instance to ask a second question such as, "Is over here all right?" This can avoid the confusion that would lead to the client's forming a negative opinion of you and/or your restaurant.

Asking and answering questions effectively is not solely a matter of effective verbal communication. Nonverbal communication (including vocal tone, facial expression, posture, and gesture) can contribute significantly to clarity and to the establishment of a positive image of one's workmanship. The key to nonverbal success in questioning a client is, again, to look directly at the person while speaking. In so doing, you communicate sincerity and interest in the client's response. This will make it more likely that the client will provide you with a meaningful response. In addition, by looking directly at the client, you can pick up his/her nonverbal messages.

The nonverbal component of the client's answer can contribute greatly to your accurate interpretation of the answer. The car owner bringing a car in for service, for example, is quite likely to gesture in trying to explain the funny noise or the drip the car is producing. Those gestures may be your only clue as to whether the noise is coming from the driver's or passenger's side of the car, or to the approximate size of the puddle made by the drip. You must be looking at the client to pick up such useful nonverbal clues to meaning.

The health care worker especially is strongly advised to maintain direct eye contact with a client. Unfortunately, many individuals are reluctant to be verbally truthful about their pain or discomfort. In order to provide effective service, you will need to perceive the nonverbal messages about pain that the client may be unwittingly sending. You should note these, and let the client know you have read something into their body language by asking such a question as, "Is it uncomfortable for you to sit in that chair?" You may or may not be able to do anything to alleviate the discomfort, but noting it enhances your relationship with the client and can provide the other members of the health care team with useful information.

Your nonverbal clarity will also be strengthened by meaningful gestures and facial expressions of your own. Since one of the purposes of work-related questions is to establish positive relationships with clients, remember that vocal tone can convey respect, friendliness, sincerity, boredom, craftiness, anger, or condescension, among other things. Use a supportive, reasonably patient, and friendly tone, and you will be more likely to receive the respect you desire from the client. There will be many working days when your patience will be sorely tested. Nonetheless, an effort to convey a positive attitude toward clients, will have results that make the effort worth it.

Much of your interpersonal communication with clients will include asking and responding to questions. These will be brief, but very important, encounters. In the way you word your questions and behave in asking them, you communicate with the client about information needed to provide good service and convey your positive attitude toward that service. Having that information and the client's trust will lead not only to good service, but also to job advancement for you.

Social Conversation

Some of the interpersonal communication in which you engage on the job will not have the information-gathering purpose of the kinds of questions described above. There are many situations in which the goal is simply to pass the time pleasantly with the client in such a way as to establish a positive relationship. In such situations, your communication is known as social conversation.

You may be thinking that it is primarily people in cosmetology who need to engage in social conversation as part of their job. While it is true that beauticians and barbers do spend a good portion of their working day chatting with clients, they are not the only workers who do so. The health care worker will often engage in conversation with a client to fill time between procedures; the carpenter or electrician will be expected to join in conversation while making repairs in a home or office; the auto mechanic rescuing a stranded motorist should be prepared to chat during the tow back to the shop; and the appliance service technican will find social conversation with the homeowner helps to make the time pass quickly and to establish a mutually supportive relationship with the client.

Since the type of communication we have described is fundamentally a conversation between strangers, the topics for conversation should be rather general and nonthreatening. Examples of appropriate subjects to introduce would include (You guessed it!) the weather, current news, sports, seasonal topics, or the job you are engaged in. In raising such a subject, you should open with a question phrased in a way that does not put your client on the spot by forcing him/her to give serious contemplation to the issue. A client does not come into your work setting to engage in "heavy" or complicated discussion.

In addition, some of the situations in which you will engage in social conversation are stress-producing times for the client. Waiting for novocaine to take effect or enduring the drive back to a service station where one's towed car may have to undergo an expensive repair are not settings in which we will want to discuss the merits of socialized medicine or tax reform. Yet, an easygoing conversation about the fortunes of the local football team may be just the thing to relieve the stress a little. Remember that your goal in social conversation is simply to help pass the time, creating a pleasant atmosphere for the client and yourself.

The direction of a conversation should be dictated by interests expressed by the client. In your role as the service provider, you must be attuned to the client's interests and sensitivities. This means that you should keep the discussion at a general level unless the client responds in manner that suggests a more personal discussion is appropriate.

You might open the conversation by asking, "Is it still snowing out there?" The client who does not wish to engage in much idle chatter will respond with an answer of few words. In that case, your response should again be general. However, if the client answers by commenting on how the current weather has affected his/her life in a personal way, then you are justified in pursuing the conversation on a more personally relevant level. For instance, the client's answer about the snowy weather may include reference to the difficulty experienced in trying to get his/her daughter to cheerleading practice the previous night. With that opening, you could respond, "Oh, your daughter is a cheerleader? That must keep you busy." The conversation could then proceed in this somewhat more personal vein.

Avoid taking the conversation in the direction of focusing on elements of *your* personal life however. You are a stranger in the client's "home." The client will be uncomfortable in talking about your family, hobbies, and so forth. In addition, the client is paying you by the hour and will resent spending money while you chat about your life instead of working.

In other sections of this book, we have stressed the importance of being well organized in speaking, having all ideas as fully developed as possible and clearly interrelated. While those are very important guidelines for the more formal speaking situations, they do not apply to social conversation in the same way. Since the client sets the depth and pace of the discussion, some ideas may indeed be fully developed while others get only minimal attention. That is perfectly acceptable in informal conversation, and you should be flexible in your contributions to the conversation to allow for such variations.

Moreover, to you, some of the client's comments may not seem clearly pertinent to the topic. If any such comment had occured in a more formal setting, you would have asked the person how it related to the idea under discussion; not so in social conversation on the job. You should just acknowledge the comment with an affirmation such as "Oh, really?", and continue in the new direction of the discussion. Your role in the conversation is to be supportive and make the client feel comfortable, not to be a critic.

While there are no hard and fast rules for conversational success, the suggestions presented here should help you to participate in a satisfying way in the casual conversations which are necessary to working with clients. If the experience is satisfying for the client and you, your interpersonal skills will have contributed to your job success and advancement.

Telephone Talk

Not all of your conversations with clients will be face to face. There are occasions in almost any job when the telephone must be used. You may need to place an order, to clarify one, to inform a client that a job is finished, to let the client know of a problem or delay with the job, to respond to client questions, or to take a message for someone else. No matter what the specific task, certain rules of telephone courtesy must be observed.

First and foremost, enunciate your words clearly. Since the other person on the phone cannot see you, there is very little noverbal communication to assist in the interpretation of your words. If you say, "This is Joe from Snxklpz Motors; I need to qwrtps a snkjhyr," you are in deep trouble. You have mumbled to the extent that the listener does not know exactly who you are or what you want. Consequently, you now have a strained relationship with this person after only a five-second communication.

Some tips to keep in mind to enhance your articulation are:

1. Hold the mouthpiece about two inches from your mouth.
2. Speak slowly enough so that the breaks between words are distinct.
3. Be extra precise in forming particularly complicated letter groups, such as the "xc" in "excruciating."
4. Be extra precise in enunciating the final consonant of each word.
5. Speak with an open, not a clenched jaw.

These suggestions are based on the realization that English is a complicated language phonetically, with many challenging spellings and pronunciations. Instead of pretending that it is easy to understand every word on the telephone, be prepared to adjust to predictable misunderstandings. Anticipate the words in your message that might be difficult to distinguish on the phone, and either say them quite precisely, repeat them, or spell out key words and names. Even some spellings can be misunderstood because the distinctions among letters one hears, but does not see, are sometimes quite minimal. The letter "M," for instance, sounds very much like "N" on the phone. So, when you provide a spelling, you may have to provide other "identifiers," such as "M as in Mary . . . ." Remember Murphy's law: if something can be misunderstood, it will be—especially on the telephone.

Since misunderstandings are so commonplace, the second rule for telephone talk is to doublecheck key information before hanging up the phone. Key information might be a part number, a date, a name, etc.; it depends on the circumstances. Do not be embarrassed to say at the end of a conversation, "Let me confirm that part number one more time please; and you say you can definitely get it here by three o'clock this afternoon?" That few seconds of confirmation may save hours of aggravation later.

A third and very important guideline for telephone communication on the job is to keep conversations brief and to the point. As we all know, in the workplace, time is money; time wasted on the telephone is time that could have been spent accomplishing the work for which one is paid. Therefore, if you are the caller, have in mind exactly what needs to be covered in the phone conversation before you dial. If you are the respondent, keep your answers as brief as possible without sacrificing clarity or courtesy.

This leads us to the final rule for telephone usage: courtesy. Because we live in such a technological age, the telephone is frequently a substitute for personal contact between service providers and clients. We no longer have the kind of lifestyles that would permit a car owner to stop by the service station and hang around chatting with the mechanic while the car is being repaired. Instead, the car owner may drop the car off at 7 A.M., proceed on to a busy workday, and only have a brief interaction with the car service manager or mechanic on the phone. It is in such brief conversations that you as a service provider must establish a positive relationship with the client.

Your telephone manners will either establish that you are friendly, trustworthy, and interested in the client or that you are cold, insincere, and inconsiderate. The difference is the difference between repeat clients and single-visit clients. So, make sure you have a reasonably pleasant vocal tone on the telephone. Attempt to establish conditions that will allow you to hear clearly so that you don't have to ask continually for statements to be repeated. Greet a caller with a personalized, "Good afternoon, Ms. Brown. . . ." If you are the caller, identify yourself personally in addition to greeting the client personally when possible. At the end of a conversation, finish with a polite "thank you" for the call or for the client's patience or understanding. Such simple courtesies contribute to the goodwill needed for any business to be successful.

Telephones are an inescapable part of our work setting. They are an enormous convenience if used properly. If used improperly, they can lead to client-relationship problems that will be very difficult to solve. You should try to make the most of Bell's invention by speaking articulately, by doublechecking key information exchanged, by being appropriately brief, and by observing rules of telephone courtesy.

Persuasion

There will be times on the job when your conversation with a client must take on a persuasive cast. We ordinarily think of persuasion as something that occurs in "formal" speaking such as political campaigns or sales presentations. But persuasion can be undertaken in less formal settings as well. In the service industry, interpersonal persuasion is actually fairly common.

Persuasion is any attempt to influence the ideas, beliefs, or actions of another; therefore, a job as a repair technician or construction worker may well involve persuasion. You must talk to the client about your proposed repair or building project, persuading the client to agree to your proposal even though it might be costly, seem time-consuming, or even appear to be a luxury rather than a necessity. Even giving job estimates could involve persuasion.

In thinking through your plan for persuasion prior to a conversation, several important truths must be taken into account. First of all, persuasion is always going to be difficult because no one likes to change his/her mind. People like to do things their own way and are reluctant to admit that somebody else (you) might have a better idea. Second, persuasion needs to include appeals to the client's intellect *and* feelings, not just one or the other. You must try to be aware of the client's particular values as you decide which particular persuasive strategies to use. Finally, you must be prepared to communicate your persuasive message in a way that reflects your trustworthiness and expertise.

Once you have thought through these basic principles, start planning what you will say. First, you must have accurate, specific information to share with the client. Let's say that you are a plumber called to investigate a slow-drain problem for a client. After conducting your investigation into the exact cause and extent of the problem, you determine that the client will need some new piping to replace old work that has become misaligned over the years. Calculate the realistic cost of the repair both in terms of the ideal way to do it and a less expensive approach that might alleviate the problem for a while. It is important to have both figures in mind so that you will appear reasonably flexible, and will show the client that you have his/her best intersts in mind.

The second step in planning the persuasion is to try to determine the client's relevant value systems. In our plumbing example, for instance, you should have been noticing some pertinent information about the general state of the house while you were investigating the drain problem. This will help you to determine how careful the homeowner is about household maintenance, and you will be able to make some judgement about whether the client would prefer the more or less expensive repair. You may notice, for instance, that the house seems a little rundown in general, yet is very clean and tidy. That would suggest that the client does wish to have a house that looks good and is trouble free, but has just fallen behind in addressing some of the effects of the house's aging.

With these observations and the factual information in mind, you can now put together your specific proposal for the client. You should acknowledge the client's values and indicate how the proposal is a nonfrivolous way to maintain those values. Our plumber might say, "You have done a good job of maintaining the plumbing in your house; but, the drains are slowing because of deteriorated older piping that ought to be replaced. If it is not replaced, the problem will get worse, causing odors and even messy backups in your sinks and tubs. The job can be done in the following way . . . . This will cost . . . . Or, you might want to consider doing . . . at a cost of . . . ."

This manner of presentation shows the client that you care as much about the house as he/she does and that you have an intelligent approach to solving the problem. Of course, if your perception of the client's values were different than that described in the hypothetical example, your wording of the attempted persuasion would also be somewhat different.

As you are making such a "pitch" to the client, remember to maintain direct eye contact and to appear self-assured and confident. Nonverbal behaviors will also help to comunicate your trustworthiness, which will be a great asset to persuasion.

In the service sector, you will get work if you can persuade clients that they need you. You should, therefore, see persuasion as an important part of your job, and persuasive communication as a set of skills to be mastered.

In this chapter, we have discussed various goals to be achieved through interpersonal communication with a client. You must be effective in asking questions and responding to the answers to get the information needed to do your job well. You must be effective in carrying on casual conversation to create a comfortable setting for the client while you do that job. You must be effective in talking on the telephone to maintain positive ties with clients who are not physically present at your job site. You must also be effective in interpersonal persuasion so that you can get jobs and so that you can establish relationships that keep clients coming back to you.

Reference to Testimonials

For further discussions of the concepts and skills presented in this section, read the following paragraphs in the **Testimonials from the World of Work (IV):**

Testimonial 1. The Value of Oral Communcation, Paragraphs 1.6, 1.8, and 1.12

Testimonial 3. Importance of Telephone Skills in Customer Service, Paragraphs 3.1-3.5

Testimonial 4. Oral Communication: A Roadblock to Student Success, Paragraph 4.3

Testimonial 5. Interpersonal Communication Skills, Paragraphs 5.2 and 5.7

Application Exercises

Objective: To demonstrate an awareness of communication skills that will enhance the success of your interactions with clients in one-on-one situations.

Activities: In a brainstorming meeting with other members of your class, develop a list of appropriate general opening questions for conversations with clients. Make sure these are questions you can ask while expressing sincere interest in the answer.

Choose one of these questions and use it to open a role-playing conversation with a classmate in which one of you plays the client. The conversation should last at least five minutes.

Then, using the telephone directory's yellow pages, select three companies in your area. With a classmate, role play a telephone call in which you represent one of those companies. Assume you are calling one of the other two companies to place an order for parts or supplies. Watch your diction to make sure that accurate information is exchanged between the two of you.

Next, assume that you are presenting an estimate for work to be done for a client. List the attitudes that you think a client (member of the public) would have that would hinder his/her willingness to accept your bid. List the attitudes that he/she might have that would increase his/her willingness to accept the bid. Using these two lists, identify the communication strategies that you ought to use to be successful in this persuasion.

Objective: To demonstrate understanding of vocal tone in telephone usage.

Activity: Read aloud each of the following sentences, emphasizing the highlighted word in each reading:

1. What time will you *be* here?
2. What time *will* you be here?
3. What time will *you* be here?
4. *What* time will you be here?

Discuss the differences in meaning implied by the four different readings. Probably, the first conveyed the impression that the speaker was excitedly waiting for the other person, while the second may have conveyed more frustration, and so forth.

Now, discuss the specific modifications in vocal tone used to convey the different meanings. Was the emphasized word spoken louder, softer, slower, at a higher pitch, at a lower pitch, etc.?

Discuss the impact of such differences in meaning by answering this question: If you are an employee at an auto shop, or a beauty shop, making arrangements to meet the caller as a client, which means of expression would be most appropriate and why?

Try a variation on the same activity with the sentence, "That will cost you $1,200." Convey the following four different meanings by manipulating your vocal expression. In other words, put the emphasis on a different word each time:

1. This is a reasonable estimate on your remodeling job.

2. This will be an additional expense incurred because you have added something to what you originally asked us to do.

3. This addition to the original job is excessively expensive. Are you sure you want to do it?

4. What you thought might save you money will actually cost you more.

Talking on the Job: Being a Team Worker

Student Competency Goals

After reading this chapter, the student should be able to:

- Explain ways in which groups are used in the workplace

- Demonstrate understanding of roles in small groups

- Actively participate in a problem-solving group discussion

- Appreciate the need for oral communications skills in formal group meetings

In today's workplace, you will be a member of a group or team of workers more often than not. That group might include three or four people working in the same capacity on a project (such as several masons working on a building), or several different types of experts contributing to a multifaceted task (such as a graphic artist, a layout designer, and a writer working together on a brochure). Whatever the circumstances, you will need effective oral communication skills to make such teamwork effective, efficient, and highly productive.

There are some built-in complications anytime we try to work effectively with others in such situations. Naturally, as with all communication situations, there is the chance of simply being misunderstood. But, in addition, members of a small group face the challenges of adjusting to one another's work habits and personalities and of dealing with the relative slowness of all group work. As members of a team, you are like cogs in a wheel—each different, but each expected to fit together with the others for smooth functioning of the whole. Thus, skill not only at perceiving others and in your relationships with them, but also great *adaptive* communication skill will be needed as you work within a team.

Communicating on the Team

When you work with others, you must first be a good listener. That involves paying close attention to what the other members of your group are saying and giving them clear feedback when they speak. Make sure your coworkers' ideas are clear to you and relate in some specific way to the overall direction of a conversation. If necessary, ask a clarifying question. Others in your group may be equally confused. Remember that in a group, everyone's ideas *must* fit together.

Such attentive, effective listening is going to be more difficult if you have any personal conflict with any other member of the team. That is, you may find a person difficult to work with because of personality, work style, or past history. Difficult as it may be, you must still work together. That will be easier if, in your communication with that person, you focus solely on the task at hand. In other words, as you listen, and as you express your own ideas, refrain from pre-judging; don't try to read a hidden meaning into his/her words; and keep all critical, personal innuendoes out of your own words and nonverbal expression.

For example, let's say that you are a mason working as part of a team building a large foundation. Perhaps the person mixing the mortar is one with whom you have worked before and have found to be difficult. That person may call out to you, "Okay, this batch is ready." Because of your prior history with him/her, you may hear those words and interpret them to mean that he/she doesn't think you are working fast enough. That annoys you, so you snap back, "Keep your shirt on. I'm moving as fast as I can." Now, in this scenario, both your listening behavior and your speaking behavior are flawed and will result in increased strain in your relationship and a less productive team effort.

Now let's turn this into a more constructive communication style. The mortar mixer says the same thing, but you listen and interpret the words with mental focus only on the task, not on your previous relationship. Your interpretation is then simply that the materials are ready whenever you are, so you call back, "I'll be ready for it in five minutes." With this response, you have not contributed any more problems to the relationship with your coworker, and you have given him/her clear, specific information that will help both of you to proceed with your parts of the job.

As you can see from this example, communicating effectively as a team member depends both on your skill as a listener and as a speaker. Your nonverbal communicaton is, therefore, just as important as your verbal communication. Your facial expression, vocal tone, posture, and gesture need to convey a positive attitude toward your work relationship with the other members of your team.

This does not mean that you should try to fake a liking for individuals that you truly don't care for. Rather, you should try to show a willingness to listen patiently to all others and to perceive yourself as a *co*worker, not an enemy. Let your facial expression appear politely and noncritically attentive; let your tone be as expressive as needed for clarity, not for criticism; let your posture be relaxed; and let your gestures contribute to, not distract from, the intended meaning of your words.

By following these suggestions, you and your fellow team members will experience the positive relationship known as *camaraderie*. It may still be that there are some group members with whom you do not personally get along; you wouldn't think of socializing with them, and so forth. However, your job-related communication has not reflected that. You speak and listen in such a way that you can cooperate and "fit together" to build the foundation, or produce the brochure, or whatever the team task is.

Committee Communication

Occasionally on the job, you will be asked to serve on a committee, perhaps a plant safety committee, grievance committee, or Christmas party committee. As with the less formal work groups discussed above, such formal committee work can be facilitated by your oral communication skills. You will need to be a careful listener and a clear speaker in order to help the committee accomplish its task efficiently.

Generally, a committee is given a specific amount of time in which to complete its assignment. The time constraint of having a room reserved for just one hour or needing to meet a short-term deadline can be quite a problem since group work, by definition, is slow. Thus, it is vital that whoever is planning the committee meeting must do so carefully.

A specific agenda should be developed to indicate the priority of particular items to be addressed at such a meeting. Enough copies of the agenda should be made so that each member of the committee can have a copy for the meeting. That way, each participant can contribute to the efficient use of the group's time by being aware of the need to resolve certain issues in order to move on through the agenda. Any member of the group (not just the chairperson) should be prepared to point out logistical or procedural needs of the group. So, having access to the agenda and feeling responsible for helping the group to monitor its progress through it are fundamental requirements for any good committee member.

As you can see, during any committee meeting, you may be speaking to accomplish one of two purposes: sharing information the group needs to solve the problems it has been charged to deal with, or making a point about the way the group is working through the agenda. For either purpose, your words should be chosen for their clarity and economy. Clarity we have already discussed.

By economy, we mean that you should state your point as briefly as possible. However, it should also be made clear how the point relates to what the group has been discussing and how it can lead to a conclusion the group seeks. It is better to say, "Just as Jan said, we need to have the party closer to December 1st. I think we could do that and save money by getting in on the deal offered by the club. Let's put that down as an option." It is too vague to say, "I think we should take advantage of the club offer."

The first way of stating the point does so in a way that clarifies how the idea fits in with the flow of the group's discussion. The second, while briefer, is going to necessitate several questions from others about why you think that's such a good idea. Therefore, the total time used to make your point will end up being greater than if you had stated your point more thoroughly in the first place.

Often, a point is best made in the form of a question. Since a committee has been formed to take advantage of the "two heads are better than one" philosophy, you should make sure that you are hearing the perspectives of everyone in the group, while doing so as economically as possible. This will require that you be perceptive of your colleagues on the committee. You will need to be aware of the special knowledge or expertise that each member brings to the group so that you can ask questions that help the committee to capitalize on that expertise. You will also need to notice your colleagues' nonverbal behavior to determine if somebody wants to say something but has been unable to do so. Sometimes discussions get so vigorous that less assertive committee members cannot get a word in edgewise.

A well-timed question on your part can solve that problem: "Joe, you look like you wanted to chip in here." Of course, questions may also be needed to clarify information or opinions expressed by your fellow committee members. Your repertoire of contributions in the committee meeting, then, should include questions and statements which contribute clearly and economically to the flow of information and to the decision-making strategy of the discussion. Remember that the fundamental reason for the existence of any committee is to reach decisions that cannot be made by one person alone. So, you should be speaking so as to help weave together the various perspectives and information of all the group members. This should lead to a definitive decision.

One of the most common errors of committees is their failure to clarify and specify actual decisions reached. Somebody in the group (again, not necessariy the chairperson) needs to speak up near the end of each part of the agenda to state the conclusion the group appears to have reached. State this clearly and simply so you can determine if your perception of the group's thinking is accurate. Something like, "Are we all agreed, then, that improving the loading dock is one of our key safety goals?" would accomplish this purpose effectively. Make sure, by your own statements and questions, that the committee does not adjourn until each decision is clarified and confirmed by the whole group. This communication strategy will increase the chances that the group's decisions will be acted upon.

Communication in Very Formally Organized Groups

The special skills appropriate in even more formal group meetings need some attention before we conclude our consideration of small group communication. The most formal of job-related group meetings are those of certain boards, unions, or commissions. In many instances, meetings of such groups are conducted according to the rules of parliamentary procedure which dictate when and how any group member may speak. Such rules can be very complicated, but they are necessary for larger groups involved in actual legislative action. The purposes of parliamentary procedure are to insure that both majority and minority opinions are heard during any deliberations, and that those deliberations run relatively efficiently.

If you belong to a group whose meetings will be conducted in this formal way, you can rest assured that the discussion will be fair *if* all the participants are sufficiently familiar with the rules of operation. You will need to know how to make a motion, how to hasten debate on an issue, how to limit debate, and how to bring debate to a close. Although parliamentary procedure in its entirety is quite complex, fundamentals can be easily mastered. Manuals such as *A Practical Guide to Parliamentary Procedure* by Strother and Shepa (Tichenor Publishing, 1983) are worth adding to your library should you become an officer of a more formally organized group.

Speaking and listening in small groups will be a significant part of your work life as a member of informal work teams, formal committees, and highly structured organizations. To participate effectively in these settings, you must listen supportively to your fellow group members; you must make comments and ask questions that help to draw together the collective wisdom of the group; and you must be attentive to the need for procedural clarity and efficiency by speaking economically and with specific reference to the planned agenda. By demonstrating such communication skill, you will be both a valued group member and employee.

Reference to Testimonials

For further discussion of the concepts and skills presented in this section, read the following paragraphs in the **Testimonials from the World of Work (IV):**

Testimonial 5. Interpersonal Communication Skills, Paragraph 5.8

Testimonial 6. Communication: The Key to Advancement, Paragraphs 6.2 and 6.3

Testimonial 10. Communicating in the Solitary World of Masonry, Paragraphs 10.10 and 10.11

Testimonial 12. Communication Means Success or Failure in Construction, Paragraphs 12.1, 12.4, and 12.8

Testimonial 13, Facing the Challenge of Communication, Paragraph 13.4

Application Exercise

Objective: To demonstrate an understanding of roles played in small groups *and* of the proper strategies to be used in problem-solving group discussions.

Activity: Divide the class into several groups of five to seven members each. Each group should select as a topic a problem they see in the school. In turn, each group will have twenty minutes to discuss the problem in front of the class and to generate an appropriate solution.

During each discussion, the other class members will identify the roles played by each group member by completing the following chart: Each group member's initials should be placed to the left of the columns, and a slash placed in the appropriate column for each comment made by a group member. Then, discuss the class's conclusions about the roles demonstrated.

Roles Played in the Group

Initials	Questioner	Information Giver	Clarifer	Supporter
————				
————				
————				
————				
————				

	Interrupter	Opinion Giver	Tension Reliever	Distractor
————				
————				
————				
————				
————				

Talking on the Job: Turning Confrontation into Communication

Student Competency Goals

After reading this chapter, the student should be able to:

- Recognize problem "ownership"

- Analyze the ineffectiveness of sending/receiving power-based *You*-messages

- Recognize the parts of a properly stated *I*-message

- Create and deliver a properly stated *I*-message

- Discuss the communication benefits of sending/receiving *I*-messages

- Create examples of *I*-messages for the workplace

Human beings talk—a lot. This does not necessarily mean they communicate. As we have seen, effective communication is something at which one must work. That is what this book is all about. Yet, all this good work can be undone when we try to confront another person whose behavior is interfering with our meeting our own needs. What can be healthy confrontation can also turn into communication-blocking conflict unless we use effective communication skills. These skills have to be learned. This chapter provides you with a specific communication skill to confront someone whose behavior is interfering with your meeting your needs. This skill works, allows both parties to "save face," and does little damage to an ongoing relationship.

When "I own a problem," I have classified another person's behavior as being "unacceptable" (interfering with my meeting my needs), and have recognized the need to confront the other person in order to get him/her to change behavior. *How* one confronts another can be the key to getting needs met. How one confronts another person can keep the lines of communication open or slam them shut!

You-Messages

When others interfere with our meeting our needs, it is tempting to communicate with power-based messages. These are called *You*-messages: "If *you* know what is good for *you*, *you* will get those blueprints done by Thursday or else!... If *you* had any consideration for *your* fellow workers, *you* would do *your* fair share of the clean-up duties." One can picture a boss or fellow worker shaking his or her finger at another person while uttering these *You*-messages.

You-messages are roadblocks to communication. Typically, these messages send solutions (*yours*, of course); they moralize; they lecture; they ridicule; they threaten; or, as in the sentences above, they may do several of these at one time. They also close off communication! *You*-messages may succeed in changing the behavior of another person, but at what cost? They often result in defiant compliance, cause the other person to "lose face," and weaken the relationship between the two of you. After all, you have won, and the other person has lost.

Take a moment and think of those times when a boss simply told you to change your behavior, sent you a *You*-message. The message said, in effect, "... do it or else." How did you feel? Did you defiantly comply? What choice did you have? Did you "lose face"? Did that hurt just a little, maybe a lot? Did you fantasize about finding some opportunity to "get even"? Did the *You*-message weaken the relationship between the two of you? Did you make a mental note to avoid this person as much as possible in the future?

You-messages imply that one is so insensitive to the other's needs that he/she *has to be told* how to change behavior, otherwise it would not happen. Is this true? If another person simply explained, without placing blame, how your behavior was interfering with him/her meeting his/her needs, might you have voluntarily changed your behavior? There is a good chance you might have. *You*-messages never give one a chance to voluntarily change his/her behavior.

I-Messages and Their Use at Work

Why send *You*-messages when a more effective alternative, called *I*-messages, exists? A properly constructed *I*-message consists of three parts:

1. A description without blame of another person's behavior that is interfering with your meeting your needs
2. A description of the tangible effect that behavior is having on you now or in the future
3. A description of the feeling that tangible effect is causing in you

The following are two work-related situations where one might judge another's behaviors to be "unacceptable." Immediately following each situation is an *I*-message designed to confront the other person, to get him or her to change behavior willingly, to allow both of you to "save face," and to do as little damage as possible to your ongoing relationship.

Situation 1: John, a fellow carpenter in your shop, regularly moves the safety guard aside on the band saw so that, when you use the machine, you have either to use it without the guard in place or take precious time to readjust it. John's behavior is interferring with your meeting your needs. In the first case, your need for safety is threatened. In the second case, your need for productivity is threatened.

I-message: "John, when you use the band saw and move the safety guard aside, I either have to use it without the guard properly installed, which frightens me; or I have to take the time to readjust it, which frustrates me because I fall behind in production, possibly costing me my bonus."

Situation 2: Joan, a kitchen worker in a restaurant, comes to work at least five minutes late each morning. The net effect is that, when the doors open at 8 A.M. and customers stream in, nothing is ready to be served: no coffee, grill not hot for breakfast orders, and so forth. The customers take it out on the waitresses, who, in turn, take it out on you. You are afraid that your boss will give you a poor six months' evaluation which, in turn, will affect the size of your expected raise.

I-message: "Joan, when you come to work late each day, we are unable to get the kitchen up and running on time. Then, the customers get upset and take it out on the waitresses who, in turn, take it out on me. This makes me feel embarrassed. Furthermore, I am afraid that I will earn a poor six months' evaluation and thus miss out on an expected pay raise.

Each of the two *I*-messages above contains the necessary three parts. For John, who moves aside the safety guard, the first part of the *I*-messages points out, without blame, the behavior that is interfering with your meeting your needs (safety guard left aside). The next part describes the tangible effect that behavior is having on you now or in the future (must expose yourself to danger or take time to readjust the safety guard). The last part of the *I*-messages describes your feelings (frightened and frustrated). Wouldn't it be tempting to simply send a *You*-message such as, "John, stop trying to show everyone how macho you are" (diagnosing); "John, a responsible worker would keep the safety guard in place" (moralizing); or "John, if you move the safety guard aside one more time, you are going to be in real trouble" (threatening)?

Why Do *I*-Messages Work?

Why do *I*-messages so often work? An *I*-messages does not tell other people how they should change their behavior. That is left up to them. They have a chance to *voluntarily* change their behavior. Further, an *I*-message does not say anything about other people; it concentrates upon you. *I*-messages tell how "you" are being tangibly affected and how "you" feel. Unlike *You*-messages for which the recipients are likely to dig in their heels and resist or fight back, it is pretty hard for other people to get defensive when the focus of the *I*-message is on yourself.

An *I*-message also communicates trust in the other person. It communicates that a relationship is strong enough so that if I state what you are doing that interferes with my meeting my needs, you will more than likely volunteer to change your behavior. Often the other person will respond to an *I*-message by saying, "Gee, I'm sorry; I didn't realize it was causing you a problem. How about if I do such and such?" How much better it is for the other person to suggest ways to change his/her personal behavior than for you, through *You*-messages, to make those suggestions for him/her. It gives him/her a chance to be the "good guy," the "hero," by choosing, rather than by being forced, to change behavior.

No doubt some will be skeptical about exposing their feelings so openly to another person. *I*-messages require one to be honest with others, and to acknowledge that others do have the power through their behaviors to interfere with your meeting your needs. This is the "tangible effect" portion of the message. When one adds to that the admission of true human feelings such as fear, discouragement, frustration, or vulnerability (the "feeling" portion of the message), this may take more courage and trust than some readers possess.

I-messages work on the assumption that you and the other person have an ongoing relationship, one that has basically been beneficial to both of you. Bosses need workers, workers need fellow workers, and so on. We all have a stake in promoting good relationships. The alternative to an *I*-message is a finger-shaking *You*-message that communicates "do it or else." You probably don't like to receive such messages, so why send them?

Will you sound a little "phoney" when you first practice sending

I-messages? Probably, but so what? If you value your ongoing relationship with other people, shouldn't they be treated with the respect that an *I*-message communicates? Will *I*-messages *always* work? The answer is definitely, "No!" Human interaction is not an exact science. We are playing the odds, looking for those skills that work with most people, in most situations, most of the time. If we had an interpersonal communication skill that *always* worked, we would bottle it, sell it, and be millionaires!

A significant side benefit of using *I*-messages with others is that, from the example, they, too, may start to use such messages as their vehicle for problem solving. Just imagine the decrease in work-related, as well as family-related, problems if we all regularly sent *I*-messages to one another.

Appreciative *I*-Messages

When using *I*-messages, an effective strategy for confrontation, problems get solved, needs get met, those involved save face, and a more open, ongoing relationship is nurtured. But, *I*-messages are not just for use in those situations where another's behavior is unacceptable to you. *I*-messages are just as useful when another's behavior is very acceptable to you. The common element in these different situations is that you possess strong feelings, negative in the former cases and positive in the latter. In either case you need to communicate these feelings, and an *I*-message can be your best strategy.

An appreciative *I*-message does just what it sounds like it should do. It expresses your appreciation of another person's behavior. Someone has done something that tangibly affects your life, and, as a result, you have strong positive feelings. You want to thank someone for his or her behavior. Too often we thank people simply by saying "Thanks." What is missing when one says "thanks" is the specific behavior another is being thanked for, a tangible effect upon you of that behavior, and an identification of your resulting feelings. What is missing are the three parts of a properly stated *I*-message.

Messages of appreciation are so much more effective when delivered in the form of an *I*-message; for instance, "When you replaced the empty cylinder of oxygen in the welding torch, it gave me more time to complete a difficult series of welds, thus allowing me to meet

an important deadline. Meeting this deadline makes me feel relieved."
Contrast this appreciative *I*-message with the more typical, "Thanks
for replacing the empty oxygen tank." Which of the two messages
best communicates what you really wanted to say? Which message
communicates greater, as well as more sincere, appreciation? Which
message would you like to receive? Which message would likely
strengthen your ongoing relationship, and, thus, communication,
with the other person? Clearly, properly stated appreciative *I*-
messages should be preferred.

Reference to Testimonials

For further discussion of the concepts and skills presented in this
section, read the following paragraphs in the **Testimonials from the
World of Work (IV):**

Testimonial 5. Interpersonal Communication Skills, Paragraph 5.8

Testimonial 8. Communication Skills in the Auto Shop, Paragraph 8.2

Testimonial 10. Communicating in the Solitary World of
Masonry, Paragraphs 10.3, 10.7, and 10.9

Testimonial 12. Communication Means Success or Failure in
Construction, Paragraph 12.5

Application Exercise

Objective: To prepare and deliver a properly stated *I*-message, and
to analyze the results.

Activity: Identify someone whose behavior is interfering with your
meeting your needs. Using the three-part grid below, create an *I*-
message that you might deliver to this person:

Description of Person's Behavior without Blame	Tangible Effect on You	Feelings

Meet with one or two other students and share your *I*-messages. Determine whether or not all three parts of the *I*-message are clearly stated. Make any necessary improvements.

Deliver your *I*-message to the person whose behavior is interfering with your meeting your needs. Meet once again with the one or two other students to analyze the results of sending your respective *I*-messages.

Repeat this exercise with an appreciative *I*-message. Discuss how both types of *I*-messages relate to bringing about more effective communication.

INJECTION MOLDING PLANT MANAGER
. . . . Must have thorough knowledge . . . and
strong management and communication
skills. . . .

DIESEL GARAGE MANAGER . . . . Excellent
opportunity for working Truck Diesel Garage
Manager. . . . *Organizational skills necessary.*

III
Communication Skills for Public Speaking

PC SOFTWARE COORDINATOR . . . requires
three years experience, . . . good oral and
written communication skills, ability to organize and conduct training classes.

DINING SERVICES MANAGER . . . must have
completed dietary manager's approved course
. . . . Successful candidate will possess *leadership and human relations skills.* . . .

Talking to Employee Groups and the Public

Student Competency Goals

After reading this chapter, the student should be able to:

● ·Understand the occasional need for public speaking
and the need for analyzing listeners prior to such speaking

● Plan a well organized, informative oral message about a
trade process

● Adapt that message to a variety of audiences

● Present the message calmly and articulately

The first level for management positions is most often that of
foreperson: having responsibility for guiding and monitoring the
work of a full shift of employees within a particular work area. Most
often, your interaction with these workers will be on a one-to-one
basis. But, there will be occasions when you must get all the workers

together for a general explanation. This now becomes the type of oral communication known as public address.

In addition, there may be opportunities for you to engage in public address when the audience is not the employees who work under you, but some group of stangers such as the new owners of cars bought from the dealership where you work as a mechanic. Even as a student, you have the opportunity to engage in public speaking if you participate in the programs of the Vocational-Industrial Clubs of America (VICA).

An example of a situation in which you might have to speak more formally to a group of employees could be when a new piece of equipment is being installed which they all will need to use. It may be the job of the foreperson to explain its operation to the workers. Such an explanation will need to be carefully planned so that you can get sufficient information to the workers in a complete and clear manner, yet in a brief amount of time. If you must play a part in a class on car maintenance for those new car owners, you must be well prepared as a speaker to the general public.

Preparing for a Speech

Preparation for any public speaking begins with careful consideration of the people who will be your audience. You need to know their interests, their backgrounds, and the amount of knowledge they have about the subject you will be explaining. Such information will help you decide what to cover, from what perspective, and to what depth.

For instance, the explanation of new equipment in our example above would need to be more basic and more detailed if the workers had never used that type of equipment than if they have. For the new car owners, your explanation of how to change oil would be influenced by your awareness that their only interest in knowing *how* to do it is to save themselves some money. They would want less background information than a group of students who are going to be graded on *how well* they do the oil change. So, always start your speech preparation by finding out about your listeners.

After this preliminary analysis, you are ready to make some choices about what to say and how to say it. Choices that could be considered keys to your success as a speaker concern the way you organize your ideas and the way you practice your speech. To look at organization first, you must begin by choosing your speech focus. Let's return to the example of a presentation on changing oil in a car. You could choose to cover the value of regular oil changes, the types of oil available, the role of oil in the engine, and the steps in an oil change. Or, you might choose just to cover the steps in the changing process and nothing else. That decision should be made on the basis of your audience analysis as described above, and in relationship to how much time you have for the presentation.

Generally, it is more useful to cover a narrow subject in some depth than to cover a wide topic only superficially. The deeper explanation will have more impact, maintain more interest, and provide more clarity for the average listener. Either way, you should make a definite decision as to the breadth of your focus so that you can proceed purposefully with the other choices necessary for a well prepared speech.

A second choice is a decision about the exact goal of your speaking. It may be that you simply want your listeners to understand a procedure, but you may want or need to pursue the more complex goal of persuading them in some way. The goals of informing and persuading listeners are approached via somewhat different strategies, so it is important that *you* are clear about your choice.

Think of your goal in as specific terms as possible, such as, "I want my listeners to understand the necessity for using an oil of different weight in the cooler climates;" or, "I want my listeners to buy the highest grade oil we offer." Choosing the second of these would mean that your speech would need to include some appeals to the listeners' values; whereas, choosing the first would require nothing more than the straightforward information.

Once you have narrowed down the focus of your speech and formulated your specific goal, you are ready to begin organizing the flow of ideas. Start this process by putting in writing all the particular pieces of information that you think are appropriate to include somewhere in the speech. Put each piece of information on a separate card so that all the pieces can be laid out for your study. We are not talking here about each sentence that you will say in your presentation, but rather each concept. For example, one card might say "differences between 30W and 40W oil," while another might say "safe disposal of used oil." With each concept noted in this manner, it is easy to shuffle the cards around to see what pieces of information should be covered together or in what particular order.

As you study that set of cards, ask yourself what are the three, or four, or five main categories into which all the pertinent pieces of information could be placed. Jot those down on paper because those will yield the three, or four, or five main points of your speech. This step is the beginning of what will eventually be an outline, and will look something like this:

1. Gathering equipment and preparing the work area

2. Draining the old oil

3. Changing the oil filter

4. Adding the new oil

5. Clean-up and disposal

Now, look again at your set of cards to decide which pieces of information ought to be included under each of your main categories. Some cards might contain facts, some might be examples, some might be statistics, and some might be funny stories related to the task you are explaining. As you study the cards, you should decide not just where each piece of information should go, but also if it should be included at all. That is, after deciding about your main points, it may become clear that some of your information isn't relevant, but could be saved for a different presentation. Don't hestitate to set aside some information if that is the case. You never need to say *everything* you know about a topic in one speech—that would be boring.

Once you have done this sorting, go back to the outline you began and fill in the specifics you will cover under each main category. Again, don't write out complete sentences, just specifics. If you yield to the temptation to write out paragraphs in your outline, you will end up with an essay instead of a speech. The ideas won't flow in the conversational manner that is appropriate for an oral presentation.

Practicing for the Speech

Now that your ideas are well organized for the presentation, you are ready for the next major part of your preparation. Recall that for any public speaking situation, the two parts of the presentation that can be considered the keys to your ultimate success are organization *and* practice.

Next, make sure that you carefully review what you have planned and organized so that you can give your presentation without excessive reliance on your notes. It is vital that you convey your knowledge about the subject to your listeners. This is most easily accomplished if you have practiced the speech out loud several times before the actual presentation. Each time you practice it, there should be a little variation from the previous time. This happens because you are rephrasing ideas or using different examples as you try out how they sound. Sometimes what looked good on paper just doesn't sound clear enough or interesting enough when you actually hear it said. Therefore, feel free to modify your plan slightly during practices until you get to a point that sounds satisfactory.

Prepare a few brief notes to have handy during the speech, just to remind yourself of the most important information you wanted to cover; but *do not read from those notes*. You will want to look directly at your listeners and speak in a firm, authoritative tone. The combination of careful organization of your information and sufficient practice to enable you to speak effectively and conversationally will lead to success as you present speeches to employees or others. The expertise conveyed by such preparation will be especially beneficial when you must make presentations as a supervisor.

Giving the Speech

This brings us to the presentation itself. Depending upon the setting in which you are speaking, you may have to adapt to a number of constraints that could interfere with your success in communicating. Poor acoustics or competing noises in the area are examples of such problems of setting. You must pay attention to such constraints and adjust your manner of presentation accordingly. You want your workers or others listeners to get all of the information, not just a few words here and there. Therefore, you will need to make maximum use of several verbal and nonverbal strategies in adaptation.

The use of visual aids is one such strategy. If what you are explaining is an actual object, such as a machine, you can point specifically to the parts you are referring to at the time. If the parts are too small to be seen by everyone at one time, you must plan some adaptation so they all can see. You might bring a few people at a time up to look at the specific part, or you might make an enlarged model that you can refer to so you only have to give an explanation once. Such equipment should be used as a visual enhancement of your verbal explanation, which will increase your clarity.

The purposeful use of vocal expression is another helpful strategy. In such public speaking situations, the speaker is expected to be an authority—and you are! You can convey that authority and assist your overall clarity by appropriate vocal expression. Speak up so that everyone can hear all that you say. Speak firmly to show that you are knowledgeable. And speak expressively to emphasize the important points of your explanation.

Finally, when giving an explanation to many people, you must make use of the valuable communication tool feedback. When listeners are in a large group or crowd, they are more easily distracted and somewhat less likely to provide meaningful feedback than if they were listening in a one-on-one situation. Consequently, you, as the speaker, must invite some feedback from them to check the degree to which they have understood your explanation. If you are presenting information about a piece of costly machinery that must be properly used by all who touch it, you cannot afford for the listeners to have only 65 percent comprehension. The best way to solicit feedback to get closer to that 100 percent comprehension involves both verbal and nonverbal communication.

Verbally, you should ask the listeners direct questions both during and after your presentation. You might ask the general question, "Does anybody have any questions?" However, you will receive more useful feedback by asking specific questions such as, "Okay, so that is how you advance the speed. Can anybody tell us how that is different from what I said about setting the speed initially?" As a supervisor giving a speech to workers, your questioning of the listeners could take place during the explanation, immediately after, and, occasionally, days later to doublecheck their comprehension. Plant safety and economy necessitate such attention to clarity.

You can nonverbally solicit some feedback as well. This can be done by your facial expression and movement as you speak. Watch the listeners closely so that you will notice change in anyone's facial expression or posture that might indicate confusion or uncertainty on their part. If you are looking at all of your listeners (continuously sweep your eyes across the crowd), they will perceive that you want them to respond. Thus, your nonverbal behavior can be said to be soliciting their nonverbal feedback.

In addition, you may feel comfortable walking as you speak. Doing so will enable you to stay in nonverbal contact with many more listeners than if you just stand still. As you walk, you may lean in slightly towards the listeners to emphasize particular points. This, too, will serve to encourage them to respond to you. Initiating and maintaining such a cycle of nonverbal message sending and responding strengthens the communication bonds necessary for understanding. This principle is particularly true in the public address situation, since listeners feel a less natural inclination to respond to the speaker than in interpersonal communication.

Motivating through Public Speaking

In addition to structured, informative public speeches to customers, the general public, or workers, as a supervisor you may sometimes need to speak to your employees for motivational purposes. Although such a situation would be considered public address since it is one person speaking to many, it is not necessarily an extended "speech." Instead, your motivational communication may consist of nonverbal communication of leadership and authority and verbal presentation of a few brief encouraging words.

For instance, you might be opening your shop back up after a vacation shutdown. It would be best for you to greet everyone as a group, welcome them back, and say something to the effect of "Let's get to work." These words should be conveyed in a positive, enthusiastic tone if you want to be perceived as a motivational leader by your workers. The attitude that you convey toward your own work will rub off on those employees for whom you are responsible. Just as your encouragement of feedback generates feedback, your encouragement of positive attitudes will generate positive attitudes.

The job of being a foreman or forewoman carries with it many important responsibilities, not the least of which is the responsibility to communicate effectively to those working under you. You will sometimes need to speak to them collectively using public speaking skills which are slightly different from the oral communication skills appropriate in a one-on-one situation. Even workers who are not yet in a supervisory position may be called upon to give a public speech. In such situations, you should plan your ideas carefully and present them in an authoritative, motivating manner, encouraging plenty of feedback in order to achieve maximum communication effectiveness.

Reference to Testimonials

For further discussion of the concepts and skills presented in this section, read the following paragraphs in the **Testimonials From the World of Work (IV):**

Testimonial 4. Oral Communication: A Roadblock to Student Success, Paragraph 4.3

Testimonial 6. Communication: The Key to Advancement, Paragraph 6.8

Testimonial 12. Communication Means Success or Failure in Construction, Paragraph 12.6

Testimonial 14. "Didn't You Hear What I Said?" Paragraph 14.4

Application Exercise

Objective: Explain a trade process both to peers and laypersons.

Activity: Each student will select a trade process such as applying hair dye, using a pneumatic wrench, mixing mortar, etc. It should be a process sufficiently limited in scope that it can be explained thoroughly within five minutes. Students then prepare an outline of the explanation using no more than five main points.

The class wil be divided according to trade areas. Each student is to explain orally, from the prepared outline, the selected trade process to the other students in the same trade area. Then, the student moves on to a group of students outside his/her trade area and gives *exactly* the same speech. The listeners in the second group are to make note of each word, phrase, and concept that they did not understand. The speaker must then modify the explanation according to those notes (overnight assignment). The revised speech will be presented for a grade in the next class meeting.

Talking on the Job: Outside Parties, Agencies, and the Media

Student Competency Goals

After reading this chapter, the student should be able to:

- Appreciate the importance of clear communication between workers and inspectors or reporters

- Provide appropriate verbal and nonverbal responses to inspectors' questions

- Identify the special challenges of speaking on radio or television

- Plan responses to reporters' questions in a manner suitable for the group represented and others listening

● Speak articulately using a microphone

While most of the talking that you must do in order to perform your job is talking either to coworkers or clients, there will be occasions when you must speak with persons less directly involved in your total job. Such persons, outside parties, have a special expertise providing them a reason to be interested in only one small aspect of your job. While you may interact with such parties on only rare occasions, such communication must be effective, for these parties can be very influential.

Inspectors and Investigators

Investigators and inspectors make up one category of persons who should be of concern to you on your job. This category would include health inspectors (cosmetology and commercial foods), building inspectors (construction), insurance investigators (automotive and construction), and occupational safety inspectors (all trades). In every instance, their job is to attest to the nature and quality of your work or work environment, but they are not your adversaries. They are your colleagues, another part of the team. Therefore, as you communicate with inspectors, keep in mind the goal of building and sustaining positive relationships. Such relationships will benefit you on your present job and build bridges for future work.

Such inspectors and investigators will initially talk with the job foreperson, but their conversation and questions will not necessarily stop there. They have the opportunity and the right to question any employee involved in the project or work area being investigated. You may be asked to explain what you are doing, with what equipment, using what procedures, and for what purpose. In answering the questions, you have a two-fold responsibility: to be sufficiently clear and detailed to satisfy the inspector's concern, and to be a fair and honest representative of your employer. Both responsibilities can be addressed by following the guidelines for effective sharing of information presented earlier. In other words, representing the company does not require you to "act a role," just to be an intelligent communicator.

Specifically, use clear technical terms in describing your work. Inspectors should be perceived as colleagues in your trade; they "speak your language." Therefore, if you are asked in the auto body shop about the dimensions of damage to the car you are working on, give the answer in metric figures, omitting dramatic descriptive terms. It neither assists clarity nor represents your professionalism well to say that the client "really smashed this one to heck." Instead, simply state objectively the part of the car damaged and the degree of damage done.

Be prepared to supplement your explanation with visual aids, that is, to show the inspector the materials you are using or the area on which you are working. A building inspector, for instance, may want to see the particular wiring being installed by an electrician or pipe being installed by a plumber. It is appropriate for you to offer to show these materials. Don't necessarily wait to be asked. Offering to show your work reflects a spirit of cooperation appreciated by the inspector and by your employer.

Your nonverbal communication can contribute to interaction with inspectors by sending negative messages also. Unfortunately, there may be occasions when an inspector finds some violation in your work. If that should happen, do not become defensive or hostile. The health inspector may stop by your kitchen on a day when you forgot your hairnet or accidentally left cleanser near the food preparation area. Neither violation will cost you your job (at least, not the first time), nor are these difficult errors to correct. Therefore, it is wisest to use a verbal or nonverbal response which reflects understanding of the problem and willingness to correct it. You may not be expected to respond verbally at all. But, certainly your cooperative spirit can be exhibited in your facial expression. A smart-alecky comment or gesture, on the other hand, *could* cost you your job.

As in all other communication settings, conversations with inspectors and investigators require good listening skills as well as good speaking skills. Your listening should be respectful and attentive. Inspectors have the power to stop work on the job in which you are involved. Your listening manner should be fundamentally characterized by trust. Show that you trust the inspector's judgment, and he/she is more likely to show that you are trusted to make the requested modifications.

Look directly at an investigator during the conversation. Direct eye contact will establish that you have interest in what is being said, and will help you to comprehend more fully the information being given or requested. The general principle about eye contact is true here: a person who can look another directly in the eye during a conversation is a person worthy of trust.

Being a good listener means evaluating what is being said, and that can't be done if you don't understand something. So, if any of the inspector's words are not clear to you, ASK! A well-phrased question will save both of you time and aggravation because it will lead to increased clarity.

One final point should be made about communicating with inspectors and investigators. While your manner should communicate respect and attentiveness, you should not convey a sense of being intimidated by the interaction. It is easy to *feel* intimidated because of the difference between your stature or power and that of the inspector. But, do not think too lightly of your role in the situation. You are still a trained professional whose opinion in the conversation matters.

If your manner is characterized by polite directness and forthrightness, you will reinforce your professionalism in the mind of the inspector, and thereby enhance the credibility of your opinions. On the other hand, if you speak with lowered eyes, in quiet tones, and with few words, your manner reflects a lack of faith in your opinion. The inspector is likely to interpret your opinion or information with a comparable lack of faith.

In summary, when you are questioned on the job by a representative of a government agency, an insurance company, or a lending agency, listen carefully and respectfully; answer fully and in technical detail; use supporting nonverbal behavior; avoid defensiveness; and communicate a faith in yourself and your ideas.

Media, the Union, and You

A second type of outside-party conversations in which you might become involved on the job is with the media. It may seem incredible to you right now as you sit in your classroom, but you may someday be interviewed on radio or television. The interviewer in that situation would be considered an "outside party" as we have defined the term in this chapter.

The most common cause for tradespersons to be interviewed by the media is their role in a union. Because union negotiations are newsworthy, those involved (including lawyers, corporate spokespersons, union presidents, *and* shop stewards) are often interviewed. In such circumstances, unlike the case of talking with inspectors or investigators, you are speaking as a representative of the union—your peers.

Several suggestions about oral communication in general need to be reinforced as pertinent to such media situations. First, let us recall the importance of feedback. Feedback is the listener's verbal or nonverbal response to a message received. It assists the speaker in modifying what is said so as to be more clear and effective. Thus, receiving and responding to listener feedback is important to anyone's communication success.

The problem with feedback during media interviews is that your *real* audience is not physically present to give you feedback while you are speaking. Your real audience, after all, is sitting at home watching this interview on television or listening to it on radio. So, your union peers or the company management may be responding in various ways to what you are saying, but you don't know it. Naturally, this makes it impossible to modify your words to be more clear or to speak more appropriately. Therefore, those words must be even more carefully planned than in other communication settings.

Another general communication principle of specialized significance in media communication is the importance of coordinating verbal and nonverbal messages. The general "rule of thumb" is that your gestures, posture, movement, tone, and facial expressions should send messages that are consistent with the message being sent by your words. The nonverbal messages should amplify and clarify the points you are making verbally. As with receiving feedback, appropriate nonverbal communication assists the achievement of your communication goals.

In media interviews, however, you will not always have full use of nonverbal tools. A television interview may show you only from the shoulders up, reducing any expressiveness achieved with gestures or posture. A radio interview, of course, will enable you to capitalize only on vocal nonverbal messages; visual nonverbal expressions are absent altogether. Consequently, the verbal expression of your ideas and feelings will essentially have to stand alone. The influence you hope to achieve will come from the words, so they had better be carefully planned and presented.

With these general constraints as background, let us proceed to the specific communication strategies to be effective in a television or radio interview. These strategies encompass both the preparation and the presentation of your ideas. Since you will be speaking as a *representative* of a group, the first step in preparing to speak is to find out what the others think and believe so that you can represent their ideas fairly. If you have been elected shop steward or to any other union post, you must have a relatively good relationship with your peers. Think about that: what is it about you that makes the others trust you? Probably, you have similar values and concerns. Before agreeing to be interviewed by a reporter, though, you had better check that out. Ask your local's members if you are right in assuming, for instance, that they see the key issue as working conditions. Even though the members have put their faith in you, it would be inappropriate and risky to *assume* you know exactly what they think. So, ask!

The next step in preparing to be interviewed is to narrow the range of issues you wish to discuss. In most cases, you will be interviewed for several minutes, but the on-air version of the interview will be much shorter. Therefore, you would be wise to plan for the one or two points that are most important to make to the public. That way, those points can be the focus of everything you say in the interview, assuring that, even when the interview is trimmed for broadcasting, your key points will be aired.

As an example, the union may want to establish its opinion of management's handling of negotiations, the support being received from other locals, the most important contract demands, and progress of the negotiations, as well as their plans in the event negotiations fail. A typical broadcast of an interview excerpt will not permit development of *all* of those ideas. So, plan ahead by preparing a written statement to be given to the interviewer that covers all of those points in detail *and* by preparing oral comments that emphassize the most important of them for the viewing audience. This will provide the interviewer with a full, complete explanation of all the issues which he/she can use as the basis for narrating the news story into which a piece of your interview, emphasizing the most significant issue, can be inserted.

The final step in preparing for the interview is deciding exactly how to say what you want to say. Because of the special constraints on communication in the media interview, which we addressed earlier, your *exact* words ought to be planned ahead. This differs from the recommendations we have given for other forms of public communication in which we said to plan your ideas, not necessarily the exact words. The lack of feedback and nonverbal communication necessitates a change in this communication strategy. Think carefully about what words are most appropriate. Would it be better to say the union "hopes" for certain requests to be met, or the union "demands," or some other verb? Remember that you will not know what reaction those words get until after the broadcast. If you have chosen the wrong words, it will be difficult to repair the damage later; best to plan ahead to prevent damage.

As to the presentation of your ideas in a media interview, the goal here is also clarity. If your advance planning has been focused on achieving clarity, you should be able to accomplish that goal fairly easily. Your words have already been planned, so then your task is to listen carefully to the reporter's questions, select the most appropriate answer, and speak articulately.

A reporter's questions are likely to be the basics: What does the union want? How are negotiations progressing? How far is the union willing to go? However, the questions asked are not necessarily going to be phrased exactly that way. This is where listening carefully enters. Identify, as you listen, which of the basic questions you are being asked. You will have planned answers to those questions in advance. So, as you are listening, you are playing a mental "match game," mentally determining which of your preplanned answers is best for (matches) the questions asked. That is the answer to give.

Generally, it is best to stick to your planned responses. The reporter may ask some follow-up questions or may ask a question in such a way that you are put on the defensive. In either case, remain calm and simply reiterate your original answer. The reason for doing so is to keep the interview's focus on the priorities as you and the union you represent see them. Maintaining that focus increases the likelihood that the interview as broadcast will represent your views fairly.

Your articulation during an interview must be especially precise. Depending on the quality of the station's technical equipment, some sounds could be distorted or unclear if not enunciated effectively. Words with several "s" sounds in them, for instance, are often garbled. If the "s" has a whistling effect, it can blur the other sounds within the word. Speak slowly and precisely so your words and, thus, your ideas can be clearly understood.

We have defined outside parties as persons with whom you might have to communicate about your job, but whose role is somewhat removed from the actual accomplishment of your job. While they are not directly involved, such people as inspectors, investigators, and reporters have significant power relative to your job. In such oral communications, you are also typically speaking *for* somebody else (your employer or your union), not just for yourself. Therefore, while most general oral communication principles apply, there are some special tools to be used in addition. You will need to pay especially careful attention to the purposes and goals of the group you represent in speaking. You will need strong use of nonverbal communication when this is possible, and ability to adapt to a lack of nonverbal expression in other cases. You will need to use words carefully chosen for the particular impact they will have on the outside party and on the greater "audience" he/she represents. By effectively addressing these needs, you should be successful in this type of communication.

Reference to Testimonials

For further discussion of the concepts and skills presented in this section read the following paragraphs in the **Testimonials from the World of Work (IV):**

Testimonial 4. Oral Communication: A Roadblock to Student Success, Paragraph 4.6

Testimonial 8. Communication Skills in the Auto Shop, Paragraph 8.7

Testimonial 12. Communication Means Success or Failure in Construction, Paragraphs 12.2-12.4

Testimonial 13. Facing the Challenge of Communication, Paragraph 13.2

Application Exercise

Objective: To present yourself clearly, competently, and responsibly as a representative of your union.

Activity: Write a one paragraph statement summarizing your class members' reaction to the following announcement from the administration: "The class has performed such high-quality work that we will finish all the assignments one week ahead of schedule. During the remaining week, students will have the opportunity to do work for extra credit, but, since the buses and cafeteria will not be operating, you must provide your own transportation and lunch at your own expense."

This is the sort of "good news/bad news" announcement to which you might be asked to respond as a union leader or representative. In preparing your statement, follow the guidelines for such speaking described in this section. Each student should then read his/her statement to the class and be prepared for follow-up questions from any class member or the teacher playing the role of media reporters.

IV
Testimonials
from the
World of Work

Testimonials from the World of Work

    This section contains a number of brief testimonials or statements acknowledging the value of oral communication skills in the world of work. These testimonials have been written by a variety of individuals who have one thing in common: all hold positions which have made them expert observers of the impact of oral communication in the workplace. These people have credibility; they speak from years of experience in the world of work. They include, among others, a Director of Education and Training for GTE Telephone Operations, a personnel consultant to the construction industry, a journeyman mold maker, a retired master mason, and a beauty shop owner. These people have worked all of their lives with new employees, or employees in training, in vocational-technical trades. They have hired, fired, supervised, and evaluated employees. But, most of all, they have been successful in communicating with people.

How to Use the Testimonials

There are at least two ways to use these testimonials. You could simply read each person's testimonial in order to learn his or her argument for the importance of oral communication skills. After reading all, or most, of the testimonials, you should come away convinced that oral communication skills are required of all workers in general, but for vo-tech school graduates in particular.

Another way to use them is to read just those portions of one or more testimonials that specifically relate to the section of this book you are currently studying. To assist you in doing this, each section concludes with a *Reference to Testimonials,* whereby you are directed to specific testimonials and to specific paragraphs within these testimonials. Each testimonial is identified by number, and each paragraph is numbered in sequence within each testimonial.

Once again, the testimonials are designed to help convince you that oral communication skills are needed by vo-tech graduates to obtain a job in the first place and to advance once employed. Sure, this text says oral communication skills are needed. Sure, your teacher says oral communication skills are needed. Now you have a chance to hear (read) this same message from those in the know!

The Value
of Oral Communication

Tommy J. Walter
Director, Education and Training (North)
GTE North Incorporated
Westfield, Indiana

(1.1) Communication. What a simple sounding word. Yet, there are few activities in our personal and professional lives that are more important. From a simplistic point of view, there are three types of communication: written, oral, and nonverbal. Any or all of these are used minute by minute as we interact with other people.

(1.2) What seems so strange about communication is that even though it is constantly used in all aspects of our life, few of us do it really well, and many of us do not realize its importance to us. Several years ago, I was teaching a high school sophomore English class and was having difficulty inspiring one young man to do his work. Perhaps we were not communicating. Finally, in exasperation, I asked whether or not he recognized the need to be able to read, write, and speak with some degree of skill. I shall never forget the young man's response. He did not need this stuff. He was going to be a mechanic, and mechanics did not need to be able to do all that. They just needed to be able to fix cars.

(1.3) Once he responded, I was able to list many situations where, indeed, mechanics needed to be able to read, write, and speak. Perhaps his perspective was changed, and we were able to communicate, because his grades improved. However, the sad part is that then and even now he is not alone in his thinking.

(1.4) Now move forward several years to the highly technical world of telecommunications. The challenges and avenues for communication have never been greater. Technology is exploding, and the ability to apply that technology is contingent upon the ability to read, speak, and write, and the impact of nonverbal communications. The reading comes into play as employees interface with highly sophisticated computers, by reading printouts, and reconfiguring, repairing, or maintaining the device. An employee might also be required to read blueprints, repair manuals, and customer orders.

(1.5)Speaking comes into play in several ways. Employees must be able to communicate their thoughts to other employees and their specific supervisor. Also, and extremely important, some employees interact on a daily basis with customers. These interactions can take several forms, from a retail sales call to a trouble report to an angry customer. Each of these requires special skill on the part of the employee to handle the situation positively.

(1.6) One aspect of oral communications which is often times overlooked is the skill of listening. Most people are so busy thinking about what they are going to say next they pay little, if any, attention to what the person speaking is saying. This can be a devastating weakness, particularly when dealing with an unhappy customer or being faced with personal criticism, such as from one's supervisor.

(1.7) Nonverbal communication becomes important in face-to-face situations where the old adage "actions speak louder than words" takes on new meaning. An employee speaking to another employee can convey many messages beyond those carried by the spoken word. The facial expression, position of the body, and use of gestures can give dozens of clues relative to emotion, credibility of the person speaking or the one listening, and degree of interest in what is being said. The same clues are passed between a customer and employee engaged in a conversation. A customer can quickly sense the concern of an employee from the look on the employee's face.

(1.8) Of the three major methods of communication, probably the most used is spoken communication. It occurs in many types of situations, including face to face, television, and telephone. Perhaps it is the most effective in that it involves both verbal and nonverbal stimuli, and it involves listening as well as speaking.

(1.9) The ability to orally communicate is a critical skill in the business world. Not only do employees need to be able to transfer information back and forth to each other, but the ability to present one's point of view regarding an issue is essential. For instance, in the job interview, prospective employees are literally selling themselves to prospective employers. The person being interviewed can have the greatest talent available, but if he or she cannot communicate relative to his or her capabilities for the job in question, the opportunity may be lost.

(1.10) Another typical situation occurs when a supervisor talks to an employee about the employee's work performance. The employee needs to be able to listen carefully to what is being said, to clarify points made and to ask questions regarding his or her performance. Otherwise, questions or bruised feelings may remain only because communication was not as effective as it might have been.

(1.11) A third such situation occurs when an employee has a great idea to improve a work process. If the employee is unable to explain his or her idea in clear terms, both the company and the employee lose. The company forfeits because of lost efficiency, and the employee may sacrifice because many companies have suggestion plans which pay monetary rewards for ideas from employees.

(1.12) Another relevant situation is interaction with customers. Obviously, they are the reason for businesses existing. Employees' abilities to communicate with customers regarding a service problem or to sell them on a needed service are essential skills. Even more important, perhaps, are the skills of being able to ask the right questions to ascertain a customer's problem or of diffusing the anger of a dissatisfied customer.

(1.13) The question always asked about these types of skills, not unlike the question asked by the young man in the English class, is, "What's in it for me if I learn to communicate, and particularly orally communicate, better?" The answer is that, based on my experience in industry and conversations with others in other industries, the ability to rise in an organization hinges on the ability to communicate as much as on any other single skill.

(1.14) An employee can have the greatest technical skill imaginable, but the lack of ability to communicate regarding that skill will be a deterrent in his or her career. What is regrettable about such a situation is there are so many avenues available to improve the skill.

Therefore, there is a lot depending on the ability to communicate well: A person's career could depend on it.

Testimonial 2

The Importance of Oral Communication Skills in a Capstone Co-Op Program

Kenneth T. Skonieczka
Co-Op Coordinator
Erie County Technical School
Erie, Pennsylvania

(2.1) The Capstone Cooperative Vocational Education Program (co-op) at most vocational-technical high schools places seniors having requisite job entry skills with employers for further training in their chosen field.

(2.2) The major difficulty in a co-op program is the academic deficiencies of students in subjects outside of their chosen career areas. The students work very hard to learn the competencies needed in their chosen trade because they like what they are doing. These vocational competencies and skills make seniors attractive to employers, but quite often our seniors fail to communicate orally what they have to offer to employers.

(2.3) These fine young adults quickly learn as seniors that they must learn "packaging" skills if they wish to participate in the co-op program. The product they are selling to employers is a corporation known as *You, Inc.* The first co-op seminars our seniors go through deal with interpersonal skills. Our seniors learn how to make *You, Inc.* attractive to employers.

(2.4) The seniors are made aware of the fact that they may change jobs five to ten times during their lifetimes (depending upon the government statistics used). They are taught to communicate in an interview and to answer the basic question, "Why should I hire you?" We have had the experience in our co-op program of employers who interview three of our students, and the least qualified is hired simply because this particular student did a better job in the interview of orally selling himself or herself. Students quickly realize they need to improve their communication skills before they go on their first real co-op work experience.

(2.5) Once the students are on co-op employment, job-related training maintains a focus on communication skills. We have learned from the past sad experiences of some seniors and graduates who have lost jobs. Most do not lose jobs because they lack skills in the field. They lose jobs because of poor interpersonal skills. The seminars conducted after a student is on a job place emphasis on relearning listening skills, following directions, asking questions, and, in general, orally communicating on the job to keep the job.

(2.6) We have had the pleasure of working with English teachers in the past who attempted to make their courses more meaningful to their students taking vocational programs. Employers falsely criticize educators for not teaching skills needed in the workplace. The skills were taught, but the students did not transfer the skills learned to the workplace.

(2.7) The big success stories in our program are from the efforts of the vocational and academic worlds working together. Our students quickly find out on the job that they are in the same boat with their co-workers and supervisors. By working together they can solve many problems. We in vocational and academic education must also realize that we must work together.

(2.8) The world of work is where all of our students will spend the next 40 to 50 years. Today's new technology, which we hear so much about, is just one factor which will bring about rapid change in the working world. Communication skills are essential if successful training is to take place for our present and future work force as they adapt to new working environments. Our nation is in a race with worldwide competition. We must be successful if we wish to maintain our standard of living. Education will be a key to keeping our nation competitive. Only an integrated vocational-academic approach, with a focus on the working world, will be successful.

Importance of Telephone Skills in Customer Service

Nathan P. Spears
Customer Service Representative
Gates Rubber Company
Livonia, Georgia

(3.1) The main rhythm of my workday involves good oral communication skills. More than 95 percent of my customer contact comes from either telephone or written communication. During a typical eight hour day, I spend approximately 65 percent of my time on the telephone. It is very seldom that I meet clients in a face-to-face situation. This moves the abilities in listening, comprehending, and oral relaying of information to the top of my job skills list.

(3.2) Through listening, I must identify exactly what the customer needs, and then locate the information necessary to answer quickly and accurately questions that have been asked. Even the simplest request could result in customer dissatisfaction if I have not clarified and understood exactly what I have heard. For example, one of our main product lines of industrial belts is sized in widths of A, B, C, D, or E, followed by a number which indicates the length of the belt. Due to the similarity of the sound of the letters, it is easy to misinterpret what a customer said. A B134 belt is not interchangeable with a D134 belt. If I send the wrong belt, I've not only wasted time and money, I've also lost the confidence of my customer.

(3.3) Common factors that affect what I hear are the customer's accent, speech speed, and clarity of enunciation. Also, the actual clarity and volume of the phone connection itself play a part in how effective I am as a listener. Since the United States is such a large melting pot of people, these factors can very greatly from call to call.

Thus, a simple order for one B134 belt can be an international auditory experience.

(3.4) The relaying of information orally, either back to the customer or to someone within the company, is vital to being a good customer service representative. I also do this mainly via the telephone. Generally, questions or information that I relay to other areas within the company are technical in nature and require that I speak succinctly. When I have effectively communicated the customer's request, I can more easily obtain an appropriate response.

(3.5) As a front-line employee for a major manufacturing company, the skills of effective listening, comprehending, and accurately relaying information are vital. They help create what every company wants, a satisfied customer.

Oral Communication: A Roadblock to Student Success

Debbie Reznor-Douglass
Director of Education and Training
Lord Corporation
Erie, Pennsylvania

(4.1) Lack of oral communication skills is the biggest deterrent to securing and subsequently achieving success in a job. I can truthfully say that 90% of employer complaints in regard to vocational students can be directly attributed to inadequate oral communication skills, i.e., following and giving directions or handling customer orders in person and by telephone.

(4.2) I have been affiliated with vocational education for fifteen years, ten of which were direct contact with employers through cooperative education programs. My focus on the need for increased oral communication skills is based on employers telling me that students cannot market themselves successfully, and it is not due to their lack of entry-level trade skills. It is directly attributed to their lack of personal salesmanship; they can't master the "etiquette" of job seeking. An effective salesperson "reads" the person they are communicating with and phrases their comments accordingly. "Like, uh, I need a job, man," doesn't cut it with hiring personnel. Students need to talk the language of job seeking, i.e., display interview skills, not the terminology and verbiage decipherable only to the teen population.

(4.3) A second aspect of needed oral communication is when the students must work with customers by explaining procedures, taking orders, handling complaints, or giving estimates. Every employee is a representative of the company for which he/she works. If the employee can't speak, or portray the company policy and "personality," he/she actually becomes a detriment. Oral (and nonverbal) communication is a keystone to competition and free enterprise.

(4.4) Employers want to hire people who can get along with others. I see a direct corollary between good human relations skills and good communications skills. If you can't communicate what you really mean and talk openly, how can you expect to avoid personal conflict with people? I used to take examples of problems that arose, or might arise, in the work setting and have students try to resolve the problem, then go back to its roots and determine how the problem could have been avoided. Invariably poor communication of some nature was identified as at the root!

(4.5) As I review some of my comments here, I realize that, even though I didn't give specific examples, I've portrayed the feeling of frustration that I have gathered from hundreds of people telling me of incidents that center around poor communication skills. I think back on the worksites I have visited for the sole purpose of meeting with students and employers to try to mold a trainee to be accepted by society.

(4.6) I have flashbacks of myself in body shops, retail establishments, machine shops, law offices, restaurant kitchens, etc., with people in coveralls, suits, uniforms, both male and female. Every flashback carries with it a young face, naive to employment graces, with eyes directed to the floor, and me saying, "What do you perceive as being wrong, and how could you have handled it differently?" And do you know what? I got the same response from everyone—"I don't know."

(4.7) And kids think they don't need English. Move over Shakespeare; make room for Speech and Communciation!

Interpersonal Communication Skills

Lisa Borgia-Carlin
Owner/Operator
Hair Flairs by Lisa
Erie, Pennsylvania

(5.1) I will begin this testimonial by discussing the importance of communication skills. On an interview, these skills may be a deciding factor in whether or not one is hired. As a business owner, I have often not hired a person who could not practice good communication skills during the interview. The person I hire would be dealing with the public on a daily basis. They would be answering the phone, talking to customers, and occasionally handling complaints. This is all accomplished by communicating. Therefore, the manner in which this person communicates with the customers would have an effect on my business. A person with poor communication skills could really hurt the business that I have put "my all" into. A business that has taken a lot of time, effort, and money could be damaged by one employee who has poor communication skills! Word of mouth is a vital (not to mention free) means of advertising.

(5.2) If a customer has been treated poorly or is dissatisfied with services, the business suffers. Through poor communication, a customer may have thought the stylist was doing one thing when, in fact, he/she was doing another. This would cause confusion and could result in the loss of a client. Through communicating, this dissatisfied customer may spread the word to people who might have been future clients. Speaking may not have been the only problem; maybe the employee just didn't listen.

(5.3) Listening is a very important factor for both employee and employer. An employer must be able to listen to employee complaints and understand them, so that happiness and enthusiasm can be maintained in the workplace. An employee must be able to listen in order to follow directions given by the supervisor or the person in charge. Following directions completely and efficiently can show an employer that you can be a real asset to the business. This will also make for a better professional relationship. First, however, an employee must be able to clearly understand the directions. As you can see, listening and understanding directions so that you can act accordingly is all the result of communication skills. No matter how far you go in your career, whether you are owner, operator, or both, these skills are absolutely necessary.

(5.4) Good grammar aids the practice of good communication skills. Speaking concisely and clearly limits the chances of damaging the lines of communication with confusion or misunderstanding.

(5.5) Asking as many questions as possible can better educate a person for a career that one can never know too much about. There is no end to the knowledge to be learned about different areas and aspects of your profession. Keeping up to date on the latest facts is all accomplished through listening, speaking, and understanding when you go to a class or seminar. Without these important skills, you will not be able to improve yourself or move up in your career.

(5.6) Personal appearance also plays an important role in your professional career. Because the way you dress tells a lot about you, you will want to make sure your appearance sends the right message. Someone dressed unprofessionally will not make another person want to listen to what the professional has to say. A person professionally dressed for work will have a much easier time convincing someone else that what they are saying can be very valuable and helpful. In the cosmetology field, for instance, you as a stylist are a trend setter. Your clients look at you to see how you are dressed, how your hair is cut, and, most importantly, how you present yourself as a professional. From this "look," the customer will decide whether he/she will trust your judgment. After all, convincing the customer that he/she needs your professional services is your main goal. To completely satisfy them on their first visit will make them seek additional service in the future. This is what keeps a business going. Remember, personal appearance is also going to be the first thing you are judged on in an interview. You must first be hired by a professional in order to become a professional yourself.

(5.7) Requesting information from your customer is necessary so you can truly deliver the most professional service possible. On the first visit to my shop, for instance, the first thing a customer is asked is his/her name, address, and phone number, so we can keep these on file in case of an emergency. Sometimes a stylist requested may become ill, and we would need to reschedule the appointment. We also like to use these files to inform our loyal customers of special discounts and sales we are offering. Later, more information is requested when the stylist is trying to understand what the customer wants and expects from his or her visit to the business. This must be done in a very professional manner because knowing what will please customers is your main goal. A satisfied customer will be a repeat customer, and, as we all know, the more of such goals we fulfill and customers we satisfy, the more we will succeed as professionals. When dealing with the public, the information we receive must be kept confidential. Repeating important or personal information can be extremely damaging to your business and to your reputation as a professional.

(5.8) Establishing a good professional relationship between you and your employer, other employees, and the public affects everyone who comes into your business. If a customer walks into a shop where the workers are not getting along or not cooperating with one another, the customer will pick up on this and will feel the tension in that shop. This would make for a very uncomfortable visit for that customer, and he or she will not visit again. A customer walking into a shop with friendly greetings and smiling faces will feel that there is teamwork and cooperation among all staff members. This will make for a relaxed atmosphere and will set the tone for the rest of the visit.

(5.9) Showing respect between staff members and their supervisor will let a customer know that they will receive quality service because all the employees are working together as a team. This is what will get the customer back. When the customer pays at the end of a visit, he or she is not just paying for a haircut or a perm, but also for the atmosphere and the treatment received. All of this together makes for "total" service that gains the customer's respect, while showing respect for the customer. Respect must also be exchanged between staff members and supervisors in order to create a comfortable establishment for everyone.

(5.10) Upon closing this testimonial, I would like to remind you that all these suggestions relate to the same thing—*Communicating*. Without the ability to communicate properly, you have no career. I would not be where I am today if it weren't for communicating. It was the main tool in starting and establishing my business. I only wish more of these skills had been offered to me during my schooling rather than "learned the hard way," on my own. I only hope that this has helped show you just how important communicating is during your training and when you venture out into the professional world. You are the only one who can control how well you learn to communicate with others, and this, in turn, will control how far you will go with your life and to what degree you will succeed in reaching your goals. No goal is too high: I was only 21 when I opened my business. Good luck with your career!

Communication: The Key to Advancement

Randolph T. Tauber
Tool and Die Maker
Johnson Controls
Industrial Engineered Plastics Division
Erie, Pennsylvania
(as told to C.S. Mester)

(6.1) As a toolmaker, I work in a field that is growing more and more specialized. Each toolmaker typically is assigned to a particular type of job within the company and performs that job continuously, since management believes that through repetition comes efficiency. In my case, the company is involved in the manufacture of plastic injection molds, and my particular role is to work with blueprints and raw steel to create a part of the mold that will fit with those parts made by my co-workers on the floor.

(6.2) Successful completion of that job requires that I talk with other mold makers and with the supervisor who passes on the engineers' designs to us. Each job is a little different as to how much talking is required, but no job can be done without some oral communication. In some cases, a toolmaker may find an error in the blueprints and must go back to the designer to talk about the problem. In other cases, the plan is sound and uncomplicated, requiring just minimal conversation with the other toolmakers on the project.

(6.3) The discovery of a design problem creates a situation that illustrates one communication problem in industry. That is, the toolmaker must go back to the designer to explain the flaw in the design. Designers are generally receptive to toolmakers' suggestions, but often, because of the pace of the industry, have moved on to a completely new project by the time the error is brought to their attention. Consequently, the toolmakers' suggestion is "put on the back burner" until the designer can get to it—sometimes that means never at all—which can result in a costly manufacturing error.

(6.4) This example represents the kind of communication problem encountered by a company. On a more personal level, I see communication as a problem affecting an individual's chances for advancement within a company. The toolmaker's path for promotions would be from toolmaker to foreman to general foreman to plant supervisor, and each step is tied to his/her communication skills.

(6.5) It comes down to this: those who communicate better, get noticed. If you communicate in a manner that is hesitant or makes you seem unsure of yourself, you are not creating a positive image of yourself. This is especially important if you are at the foreman level or above because a foreman has to come across as being confident of his/her skills.

(6.6) The better you communicate, the more people will take to you, especialy management. If you communicate in a way that causes management to have a positive image of you, you have a much better chance of advancement no matter what your actual toolmaking skills are.

(6.7) For example, a friend of mine started out as a toolmaker and had excellent skills. But, he also was a very good communicator, knowing how to express his opinions verbally in a way that management understood and appreciated. Over the years, he has been promoted through several jobs, and he is now a plant supervisor. He now is in a position of authority over people he once worked with who were also good toolmakers, but whose communication skills were not as strong. Those individuals' toolmaking skills will never be good enough to compensate for their lack of communication skills when it comes to being evaluated for promotion.

(6.8) Communication skills are important not just on the job, but in other areas of our lives as well. We get involved in church work as adults or activities with our children that require us to do some speaking. This is not uncommon. So, communication skills are a key to moving up within the trade and to accomplishing goals in your personal life.

Testimonial 7

True Reassurance: Communication in Health Care

Diane M. Mayo, R.N.
Pulic Relations Coordinator
Brown Memorial Hospital
Conneaut, Ohio

(7.1) Health care workers, including nurse's aides, technicians, and attendants, play an important role in communicating one-on-one with patients. While their primary goal may be to get or to give some information, a secondary goal is always to reassure the patient.

(7.2) Reassurance implies encouragement, comfort, and confidence. It is also one of the most challenging types of communication health care personnel should learn and practice. Fear, anxiety, anger, and depression are common emotional experiences during illness. True reassurance conveys respect and understanding of a patient's emotional feelings and willingness to support him/ her. Understanding a patient's emotions is a challenge for caregivers because patients don't always recognize or verbalize their own feelings. Realizing this, caregivers should have as a goal to provide patients with the opportunity to explore their feelings, and to use their inner resources to help themselves manage their problems.

(7.3) In explaining what reassurance is, I think it is helpful to illustrate what it should not be. Reassurance is not cheerful clichés, pat phrases, trite advice, or other empty words of consolation. It is not falling into the trap of changing the subject, falsifying information to "protect" the patient, or belittling a patient's feelings with comments such as, "I know just how you feel."

(7.4) True reassurance is accomplished only when caregivers convey empathy for what the patient is feeling inside as well as outside. Trying to "soothe" an anxious preoperative patient, for example, with a response of "Don't worry, everything will be all right," is not reassuring because it does not acknowledge what concerns the patient. This does not begin to address the anxiety or fear the patient must surely be feeling about the surgery and its outcome. Instead, it asks the patient to forget his feelings, to deny they exist—to adopt a "don't worry; be happy" attitude. Without the chance to sort through his/her feelings, the patient may perceive that his/her emotions are inappropriate, thus adding to the stress. It has been said that caregivers who use pat phrases at anxious moments do so as a smoke screen to protect themselves from dealing with the patient's and their own anxiety and discomfort. The same can be said for the tactics of changing the subject and falsifying information. Caregivers rationalize that using such tactics spares the patient, when in reality it heightens patient stress and spares the caregiver. When attempting to be reassuring, caregivers must be truly honest and ask themselves if they are trying to reassure their patients or themselves.

(7.5) Poorly communicated reassurance lacks compassion and support for the patient. Patients commonly feel alone and isolated in the medical system. They are kept waiting for treatment. They are often referred to as numbers or diagnoses. Impersonal machines scan and probe them. It is up to caregivers to communicate human compassion underlying true reassurance, lest we be looked upon as only technicians running machines.

(7.6) It is not possible to actually "give" reassurance to patients. True reassurance comes from within the patients themselves. If caregivers offer a safe, comfortable, understanding environment for patients, one in which patients feel accepted, listened to, and valued as individuals, they give their patients the raw materials for reassurance. Patients then can use these raw materials and their own inner resources to work through their problems.

(7.7) Patients feel reassured when they understand what is happening or what is about to happen to them. Our preoperative patient, for example, would probably have felt more reassured had the caregiver given adequate information about the surgery. Reliable information, in language a patient understands, permits more self control and increases his/her ability to cope with his/her circumstance. Medical jargon should never be used to teach, explain, or give directions to a patient or family members. A patient should never have to guess about what was explained. Adequate information helps decrease patient anxiety and communicates that the caregiver understands the illness and is there to help. A well-informed patient is a more confident and compliant patient.

(7.8) As I pointed out earlier, reassuring patients is a challenge because their feelings may be difficult to identify. To identify feelings, caregivers need to become skillful in actively listening to discern and respond to feelings. But, just how does a caregiver accomplish this? Identifying feelings takes some detective work on the part of the caregiver. The first step is to listen—with eyes as well as ears. Look for clues in the way the patients stand or walk, their mannerisms, their eye contact and facial expressions. Next listen to what is not said as much as to what is said. Then try to assign the most descriptive word to what is expressed.

(7.9) For example, a patient might make this statement to a caregiver: "They can put a man in outer space; you'd think they could figure out what is wrong with me." What emotion is the patient feeling? Is he/she anxious, angry, frustrated? If the caregiver inferred frustration, he/she might respond to the emotion by answering (stating not questioning), "You're frustrated that your tests are inconclusive." This response accomplishes two things for the patient. First, it tells the patient he/she has been listened to and that the caregiver is receptive and willing to be supportive. Second, it allows the patient to look at his/her emotions, to explore them, to recognize if they are valid. By doing so, he/she can begin to cope with the circumstances. The caregiver may have to sort through many layers of statements to get to the root of what the patient is feeling.

(7.10) Skills at reassurance, like active listening and suitable responding, are not learned from one example or overnight. They take time and practice to master. They require active participation by both the patient and caregiver. Nonetheless, reassurance skills must be learned by all caregivers who wish to be of real help to their patients.

Communication Skills in the Auto Shop

James Zajic
Service Manager
Walker Brothers Buick-Chevrolet
Edinboro, Pennsylvania
(as told to C.S. Mester)

(8.1) Automobiles are enormously complicated pieces of machinery. It's a wonder they run at all. Accepting that is a key to being successful in your work in an automotive repair shop. You as the mechanic understand the complexities of the vehicle, *but* the customer who is paying for your services does not. So, an important part of your responsibility is to be sensitive to the customer who cannot understand how a $24,000 vehicle has broken down. Such sensitivity is dependent upon and represented by good communication skills.

(8.2) It is a difficult task to explain the tough realities of car repair to customers. You may need to provide complex mechanical explanations as well as financial explanations. In small shops, the mechanic does the repair and writes up the bill. In larger shops, of course, the service writer handles the billing. No matter which role you play, you can count on having to deal occasionally with a confrontational customer. The individual is angry at the car, at the company, and maybe at you personally.

(8.3) The best communication style to use in such a situation is a respectful, patient one. The key is to treat people like you want to be treated. Look them in the eye while they are talking, and show a genuine concern about their problem. As much as possible, smile and be "upbeat." It helps if you can convey an attitude of enjoying your work and not seeing the customer's problem as overly troublesome.

(8.4) While the customer is explaining the car's problem, jot down some quick notes. A note doesn't forget; so by doing this, you will always have a record of roughly what the customer has complained about or the service requested.

(8.5) It may be very useful for you to go with the customer to the car during this explanation. Often, the customer cannot give a mechanically accurate description of the problem and will be assisted by pointing to particular places in the engine, underneath the car, etc. Remember, a good picture is worth a thousand words.

(8.6) Now that you have a sense of the customer's concern and the car's problem, you can begin your actual repair work. During that time, you should still be sensitive to certain communcation needs. For instance, the customer may be waiting for the car in an adjacent waiting room. Even though this customer has been told approximately how long the repair will take, he or she may become anxious and peek into the shop occasionally to see how things are coming along. After all, "the longer the wait, the higher the bill." Your nonverbal communication at such times should conintue to reflect that "upbeat" attitude mentioned earlier and continuing genuine concern for the customer's needs.

(8.7) During the repair period, you may also have to interact with insurance adjusters. You should be aware that they have somewhat different perspectives when looking at a broken piece of machinery. As in dealing with the customer, though, when talking to the adjuster, you should speak directly, clearly, and honestly. Being sensitive to the perspective of the person you are dealing with will help you to speak and listen appropriately and thus be successful in your work.

(8.8) In conclusion, communicating with the customer and with insurance representatives is part of your job as a mechanic. Your way of interacting with customers, in particular, will directly contribute to your company's quality of service and to your personal career success. Remember this famous adage in the automobile business: "The Sales Department sells the first car; the Service Department sells the second."

Testimonial 9

Making an Impression on the Telephone

Dee Kober
Marketing Representative, IBM
(Former State Supervisor
of Business Education)
Helena, Montana

(9.1) In addition to specific job skills, personal success in any job depends heavily on effective communication skills. Oral communication is the key to success in the workplace, both with peers and with customers. Impeccable grammar, excellent eye contact, a mental outline of a conversation, and closure are all ingredients of an effective oral communication event.

(9.2) One such event needing special emphasis in the business world is the use of the telephone. The first, and sometimes the only, contact between individuals at different businesses is the telephone call. Because there is no eye contact between the caller and the answerer, grammar and enunciation become the bases for the quality and effectiveness of the communication.

(9.3) Do not make a telephone call unless you as the caller will enunciate properly. Never use "ummm" or pause too long while looking for something without telling the other person what you are doing. Never use "gonna" or "y'know," and remember to fully pronounce the final "g" in words ending with "ing."

(9.4) Use the same inflection, tone variance, and volume in your voice as you would in a face-to-face conversation. Your call will then be more interesting, warm, and friendly.

(9.5) The telephone call on the job should be thought of as a professional contact. Therefore, it should be planned with the same degree of care that more extended interactions with other professionals are. The effective telephone call need not be lengthy, but must have the following characteristics:

1. **Timeliness:** The call should be placed at the best day of the week and time of the day for the *other* person's convenience.

2. **Opening Orientation:** Initially establish some type of rapport with the other party; identify yourself clearly; and make some reference to previous conversations that will bring this conversation into focus.

3. **Well-Organized Content:** Mentally organize your conversation or write down a brief outline to insure that all key topics will be covered. Some attention should be given to the flow of the conversation, with approprite transitions from one topic to another. The caller should also plan alternative outlines to allow for the conversation to go in different directions depending on how the other party might answer the first couple of questions.

4. **Encouragement of Conversation:** Effort should be made to solicit information from the other party. The caller should use open questions beginning with such words as "what" and "how." Open questions ask for more than a "yes" or "no" answer, and thus fully involve the other party and keep the conversation flowing.

5. **Clear Closure:** Bring closure to the call by summarizing the conversation. Such a summary might include a brief reference to the purpose of the call, the points on which the two parties have reached agreement, and some statement of the outcome or action that will be taken as a result. Thank the other party for the time involved in the conversation, showing awareness that any call is always somewhat of an intrusion into another's work.

(9.6) Workers who use the telephone for transacting business have a keen responsibility to do so effectively. Oral communication skills seem to be becoming the workplace literacy issue of the decade. Nowhere is that need for "literacy"—good grammar, organization, and enunciation—greater than in the routine workday telephone call.

Testimonial 10

Communicating in the Solitary World of Masonry

Walker J. Reaher
Master Mason and Masonry Instructor
Erie, Pennsylvania

(10.1) Construction work is known as a tough trade: You must be strong silent men and women who can outwork and outplay anyone on the job. Masonry, in particular, is a trade that works to create beautiful structures, yet is also a very lonely, quiet, solitary life. As an experienced worker in the trade, I know that many days you work all day long creating a beautiful piece of work, and the only time you have talked to anyone is during your break or lunch.

(10.2) However, in many respects, talking and talking effectively is quite important to a mason's work. These include presenting yourself well when you apply for a job, talking with the foreman on the job, and talking to recommend other masons.

(10.3) A union bricklayer looking for work will check into the union hall and talk to the business agent of that local. It is preferable to present a neat appearance, but also to wear clothes that show you are ready for work. The conversation may vary little as you ask about the availability of jobs. The bricklayer must be prepared to accept a "no" and carry on small talk to see if there is any other information to be picked up. The business agent may then say something like, "Look, kid, I told you to check back, O.K.?" Respond with a polite "thanks" and leave. Communicating well includes knowing when to be silent.

(10.4) A nonunion bricklayer will probably seek work by responding to newspaper ads either by phone or in person. Common phone etiquette must be used when applying for a job. Be prepared with a clear message in case your call is answered by an answering machine. The only way you can present yourself well on the phone is being polite and using good English.

(10.5) If you go to the job site to apply in person, be prepared for a couple of other situations. Warning signs (Hard Hat Area, No Trespassing, Keep Out) will probably be posted. They are there to financially protect the contractors working at the site. By careful observation, though, the job applicant can find the general contractor's trailer (usually one of several parked at the perimeter of the construction site) and go there to ask about work. Knock on the door and wait for an answer; but if there is no answer, you may walk right in.

(10.6) The best way to begin is by saying something like, "Good morning, I'm looking for the masonry contractor. Can you help me?" Usually someone will refer you to "the one in the white hard hat over there." It would pay to ask permission to go talk to the foreman. So, the warning signs have been breached. Another possible method for this is to carry your own hard hat to be used when you approach posted sites. Calmness, politeness, and an air of determination will allow you into most posted job sites.

(10.7) Once you are actually being interviewed by a foreman, you may have to deal with a rather gruff person. You may ask for a job, and the man you have asked snaps at you. It is usually because he is under pressure from the contractor, or because of an error on the job, or maybe even because of a family problem. The applicant cannot guess the cause, but can only be prepared to take such response in stride. You should speak respectfully and calmly. Call the foreman "Sir" or "Ma'am." If you are rejected, the best response is one which keeps your options open, something like "Thanks anyway, maybe in a couple of days?"

(10.8) Once you start working, your communiation challenges are minimal. But the two that occur most frequently are figuring out the best way to ask the foreman for a different type of assignment and figuring out how much casual conversation on the job is appropriate.

(10.9) As in all communication with the foreman on a brick job, your talk should reflect politeness, knowledge of your trade, and directness. You may want to ask for a more challenging assignment.

A bricklayer must have the proper manner to approach the foreman with such a request. You don't want to make the boss feel that you think he is not competent. Speak with both self confidence and respect for the foreman's judgment. Do your work with finesse and the boss will see and be impressed. Then when you ask for a more challenging task, you'll be likely to get it instead of the "boot."

(10.10) Engaging in casual conversation with your co-workers on the job is another delicate issue. The job comes first; too much conversation, and you will no longer be working on the job. A bricklayer must keep in mind that he/she was hired to construct a building. That's not to say you don't talk to one another. But, you don't *stop* work to talk about the party this weekend, etc. While working, talk should be such that the work goes on uninterrupted. And, if you are working on the towers of the National Cathedral in Washington, as I did, the art of conversation is put totally on hold until you are back on the ground.

(10.11) One final setting in which your oral communication skill will be needed as a bricklayer is in speaking up for others who apply for jobs with your company or on your site. When a bricklayer applies for work, the boss typicaly talks to other bricklayers who communicate their impressions. In many ways, the bricklaying trade is a closed trade; the hiring of new people is based solely on the talk between bricklayers and foremen.

(10.12) In all these situations, your success is related to the impression you give of yourself by your communication. By your bearing, appearance, and speech, you must show that you know what you are talking about, know the trade, and can do the work at hand.

Testimonial 11

Society
and Communication

Richard P. DeLuca
Director of Vocational Education
Erie County Technical School
Erie, Pennsylvania

(11.1) The value and uses of good oral communication skills are readily apparent in the professions and sales-related occupations. Somewhat more obscure are the value and uses of good oral communication skills in occupations related to vocational and technical training.

(11.2) Public lack of awareness of the value of good oral communications in various occupations does not negate the critical importance of these skills in the workplace. Communication can mean the difference between life and death, success and failure, or good or poor interpersonal relations.

(11.3) To say what you mean; to mean what you say; to understand what you hear; and to be understood are the essence of good communication skills.

(11.4) Unfortunately, little time and attention is paid to observing and improving oral communication skills compared to improving written communication. Written communication skills are more tangible, structured, and easier to evaluate. Oral communication elicits a more immediate response, relying on interpretative and decoding skills and effective listening. It is clear that oral communication is more common in our daily lives than written communicaiton; thus, more time and attention must be given to improving oral communication skills.

(11.5) We have, in my opinion, given in to the idea that oral communication improvement is a natural effect of maturing, and therefore, "Whatever will be will be." If that is the scenario, it is easy to understand the lack of educational initiatives addressing this critical skill area.

(11.6) Public attitudes and perceptions about oral communication skills manifest themselves in clichés like, "Salesmen are born, not made;" "When I'm talking, I'm communicating;" "I heard you;" "You weren't listening;" "Look at me when I'm talking to you;" "It was not what he said, but the way he said it;" "Sometimes it's more important to say nothing and appear stupid than to speak and remove all doubt;" "Speak up, I can't hear you;" "Lower your voice, I'm not deaf;" "If looks could kill, I would be dead;" "Don't speak to me in that tone of voice;" "If you brought the tool I asked for, I could have fixed your car in a jiffy;" "Who made you the boss?", etc.

(11.7) All these and more reflect society's ignorance of how oral communication skills are mastered. Good oral communication skills "cannot be caught; they must be taught." In the absence of good role models, the need is even greater.

(11.8) As Director of Vocational Education, I recognize the problems with poor oral communication skills and the consequences of missed communication in the workplace. There is a national trend to integrate more academic education in the vocational-technical curriculum and that emphasis should include strategies to improve oral communication skills. "No man is an island unto himself." We must acquire good oral communication skills for our own well being and for those with whom we interact.

Testimonial 12

Communication Means Success or Failure in Construction

Nancy Coffey
Construction Industry
Personnel Consultant
Ellicott City, Maryland

(12.1) The need for good communication skills in the construction industry covers all job categories. No one segment of building a house, an office building, or a bridge is performed in a vacuum. All phases of construction overlap and impact the next phase, and, therefore, communication skills become critical to the success of the venture. The diversity of the work force combined with the number of different persons on a job site make the communication process a challenge for all concerned.

(12.2) The nature of the construction industry requires workers to communicate with several different groups, such as

- supervisors

- subordinates

- co-workers

- subcontractors

- suppliers

- customers

- third parties (i.e., county inspectors, bank inspectors, OSHA inspectors)

(12.3) Each of these requires different communication skills. For instance, the employee typically has sporadic contact with customers and other third parties. It is critical to communicate effectively so that there is a good rapport established, and misunderstandings are avoided at the outset. However, with the other groups, everyday communication occurs, and a different approach is necessary. Regardless, all communication must be clear, concise, and understandable.

(12.4) Typically, approximately 60 subcontractors and suppliers contribute to the construction process for a house. Each subcontractor will have at least two or three workers in a unit. Therefore, the potential may be for anywhere from 100 to 150 workers in a house throughout the construction process. Communication with this large a work force is complicated and critical. The nature of the work frequently has supervisors in temporary office trailers; thus, much of the communication process is oral and informal.

(12.5) As a personnel manager for a major homebuilder, I have found that the vast majority of discipline and/or termination cases I am involved in stem from communication problems. Some examples follow:

A carpenter may inadvertently be insubordinate and disrespectful to a supervisor because of misunderstanding of instructions.

A customer service technician may not listen to the homeowner's description of a problem and therefore does not fix the problem or makes it worse. The homeowner becomes irritated with the company.

A county inspector discusses sediment control issues with the job superintendent and expects changes and corrections within 24 hours, or the job will be shut down. The superintendent does not accomplish this, not due to time constraints but rather to poor communication and poor understanding of the situation.

The job superintendent must communicate with the sales department, and sales then communicates with the customer and makes arrangements for everything from available options to walk through and completion dates. The superintendent fails to communicate the proper completion date; the customer had already made moving and settlement arrangements; and the house is not ready. The customer is angry at the company; sales is angry at construction; and no one is a winner.

In all cases, better communication would have improved or eliminated the problems.

(12.6) In the construction industry, it is common to work your way up in the ranks. Typically, the first promotion into management and away from the tool belt is the position of assistant superintendant or job foreman. The two primary new job responsibilities that come with these positions are planning and conflict resolution.

(12.7) Many aspiring supervisors fail at this point mainly because of poor communication skills. Technically the person knows the job, but is unable to communicate *and* listen effectively; therefore, he/she is unable to supervise or control the job. There is a common misconception that to be a supervisor, you must talk louder; give orders, not direction; and no longer must *listen* because it is "your way or the highway." It is important to communicate effectively so that people understand, are not offended, and can accomplish what is needed. Understanding effective communication and listening skills helps in developing sound principles of leadership.

(12.8) Communication is an essential element for success in any industry. The more interaction and exposure in an environment, the more critical communication becomes. The nature of the construction industry, with the frequent interaction and the extreme diversity, requires good communication skills at all levels.

Testimonial 13

Facing the Challenge of Communication

Steven Sceiford
Maintenance Supervisor
Iroquois School District
Erie, Pennsylvania

(13.1) As a new worker, you may wonder why you should study communication. There are several important reasons.

(13.2) To begin with, when you work with people from diverse backgrounds, you must be able to answer various questions in different ways to help each person to understand. In my position I deal with custodians, maintenance personnel, teachers, secretaries, school board members, cafeteria workers, construction workers of all types, business administrators and superintendents, as well as the tax-paying public.

(13.3) With all these different kinds of people to deal with, a simple yes or no answer to their questions is not sufficient. You have to be able to relate to them on their "wavelength," so they will be able to understand what you are explaining and use the information or perform the duties requested.

(13.4) Without good communication skills there will be problems getting any job done, along with anxiety for all parties. Do you go to your supervisors and ask them to do something, or buy some supplies or equipment, and it seems they never listen or understand why something is needed? Do you try to do a job that your boss told you to do, but all the people around you are upset that you are interfering with their jobs? If this sounds like what is happening or could happen in your life, then what you need is to be able to communicate your ideas more effectively.

(13.5) In my job, I have to start with an idea and take it to the finish or end product. In that process, there are many different kinds of people to deal with, to explain the idea to, and to establish why it is important and necessary.

(13.6) Let's start with an idea, and let me show you what I mean. Where I work as Maintenance Supervisor, we had an energy management system installed to save power usage, which would in turn save money for the district. To implement this, we cycle our air handling system so that all of our air handlers will not start up at the same time. By staggering this start up, our power consumption is lowered, cutting our energy cost.

(13.7) However, the engineers for the system did not know when they installed the system that, when the air handlers are shut off, the heat valves go to full open to keep the coils from freezing in the winter. Within a short time after installation of the system, the teachers started complaining about cold drafts in the rooms. After checking this out, I went to the administration and explained what was wrong and how it could be fixed. I was told to call the architect and explain the situation to him. When I called him and explained what was happening, he understood the problem and came up with a solution that would not cost a fortune. We then had to go back to the administration to tell them what we had come up with. They accepted the solution, and, in turn, took the information we had given them to the school board. It was necessary to let the board know what the problem was and to explain the solution in order to have the money appropriated to complete the job. During all this time, it was necessary to explain to the building principals what was happening, and to share the information they needed to be able to explain the situation to all the teachers. This kept everyone well informed and able to understand others' problems.

(13.8) In the end, the problem was fixed, and everyone went about his/her job in harmony. It took a lot of communication with many different kinds of people to accomplish this. Without good communication skills, it would have been a different story.

(13.9) You have to be able to relate to all kinds of people all through your life. Without good communication skills, you will feel that no one understands you, or wants to understand you. It is not up to them to want to understand; it is up to you to get them to understand. This is what good communication is all about.

Testimonial 14

"Didn't You Hear What I Said?"

Joseph S. Bieniek, N.H.A.
Administrator
Lutheran Home for the Aged
Erie, Pennsylvania

(14.1) The art of effective communication has grown into a sophisticated skill that has seen its importance enhanced in all areas of industry. The health care field has been no exception. Health care providers set goals and use quality standards established to deliver services not only with dignity, but to provide the highest quality of life possible. Effective communication is a vital aspect of the services provided in the daily care of health facility residents.

(14.2) In long-term care, the delivery of our services proceeds primarily from three sources: physician orders (written and oral), written care plans, and individual resident desires/needs. Without exception, staff members at all levels must depend on effective listening techniques in the performance of their job responsibilities. For instance, nursing staff members receive a verbal report at the beginning of each tour of duty from their supervisors. The information given at this time is vital to the continuation of services to residents.

(14.3) All other ancillary staff play a similar vital role in this communication process. Diet changes, room changes, relaying of family concerns, etc., all require the important skills of proper listening and the ability to communicate the information as intended. Failure to insure that such skills are practiced will result in circumstances that could place the health and safety of residents at risk. If extreme enough, these circumstances could place not only an individual staff member, but the facility itself in a legally perilous situation.

(14.4) Proper listening and communicating techniques need to be promoted early in training, not only for health professionals but in all the professions. These skills need to be incorporated, at minimum, in secondary/vocational education and continued on through post-secondary education and training. Professionals in the educational and human resources fields are beginning to realize the challenge and importance of this vital aspect of preparing students for their careers. Health care facilities have begun to develop these skills with existing staff. In-service training programs stressing the importance of quality listening and communicating are now being presented to facility staff. Professional staff developers work extremely hard to convey the positive as well as the negative results possible in the communication process. Too often, the negative results cause much anxiety and frustration to both residents and staff.

(14.5) The "ideal" of totally effective communication may be unrealistic. We in management must be open to innovative ideas and concepts about this. An integral part of that approach is to be able to listen effectively to new ideas. The skills for effective communication do not come easily. A combined effort of health care providers, human resource and staff developers, and educators will have the most postitive impact. Ways to assess and evaluate communication goals also need to be defined.

(14.6) Nursing, dietary, and maintenance staff, under the guidance of facility administrators, must work constantly to maintain effective communication with physicians, residents, and families. That involves effective *listening* as well as effective speaking; one won't work without the other.

Organizations to Consult for Further Information About Workplace Communcation

Adult Literacy and Technology Project, 2682 Bishop Dr., Suite 107, San Ramon, CA 94583; (415) 830-4200

AFL-CIO, Education Department, 815 16th St. NW, Washington, DC 20006; (202) 636-5144

American Society for Training and Development, 1630 Duke St., Box 1443, Alexandria, VA 22313; (203) 683-8100

Association for Community Based Education, 1806 Vernon St. NW, Washington, DC 20009; (202) 462-6333

Business Council for Effective Literacy, 1221 Avenue of the Americas, 35th Floor, New York, NY 10020; (212) 512-2415 or 2412

Council of State Policy and Planning Agencies, 400 North Capitol St. NW, Suite 291, Washington, DC 20001; (202) 624-5386

ERIC Clearinghouse on Adult, Career, and Vocational Education, Center on Education and Training for Employment, The Ohio State University, 1900 Kenny Rd., Columbus, OH 43210-1090; (800) 848-4815 or (614) 292-4353

Institute for the Study of Adult Literacy, The Pennsylvania State University, 248 Calder Way, Room 307, University Park, PA 16801; (814) 863-3777

National Alliance of Business, 1015 15th St. NW, Suite 500, Washington, DC 20005; (202) 457-0040

U.S. Department of Education, Division of Adult Education and Literacy, 400 Maryland Ave. SW, Washington, DC 20202-7240; (202) 732-2396

U.S. Department of Labor, Employment and Training Administration, 200 Constitution Ave. NW, Washington, DC 20210; (202) 523-6050

Wider Opportunities for Women, Inc., 1325 G St. NW, Lower Level, Washington, DC 20005; (202) 638-3143

About the Authors

Cathy Sargent Mester, M.A.

Cathy Sargent Mester has been a member of the speech faculty at the Behrend College of the Pennsylvania State University, Erie, for over 20 years. In addition, she is certified as a secondary school language arts teacher and has led many communication workshops for business and industry. Her research in the areas of communication education, vocational education, and mass media have resulted in numerous conference presentations in the United States and Canada, as well as several articles published in communication and vocational journals.

Robert T. Tauber, Ph. D.

Dr. Robert Tauber is an Associate Professor of Edcuation at the Behrend College of The Pennsylvania State University. He has over two decades of work with vocational-technical schools, first as a vo-tech school guidance counselor and then as a member of one or more vo-tech advisory committees. Dr. Tauber is certified as a physics teacher, guidance counselor, high school principal, and school superintendent. He has a strong research and scholarship record including publications in vocational-technical journals and numerous conference presentations at the state, national, and international levels. His most recent book, *Classroom Management from A to Z*, was published by Holt, Rinehart and Winston (1990).

Also available from Prakken Publications:

Vocational Education in the 1990s: Major Issues. Provides an overview of and detail on virtually all aspects of vocational education in this decade. 302 pp.

List price: $16.95; school price: $13.56

The One Day Plan for Jobhunters. An easy-to-use book designed to help the reader organize a job search and clarify career goals. 104 pp.

List price: $9.95; school price: $7.96

How to Develop Competency-Based Vocational Education. Provides a step-by-step approach to the development of competency-based programs. 170 pp.

List price: $8.95; school price: $7.16

Managing the Occupational Education Laboratory. A comprehensive approach to both the prevention and solution of common occupational laboratory problems. 240 pp.

List price: $11.95; school price: $9.56

Legal Issues for Industrial Educators. Discusses legal issues and concerns of importance to teachers and administrators in easy-to-understand terms. 176 pp.

List price: $12.95; school price: $10.36

Teacher Liability in School-Shop Accidents. Details the teacher's two-fold responsibility to prevent accidents and protect against liability. 172 pp.

List price: $7.50; school price: $6.00

To place an order or for more information, contact

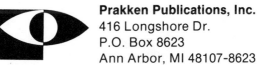

Prakken Publications, Inc.
416 Longshore Dr.
P.O. Box 8623
Ann Arbor, MI 48107-8623
(313) 769-1211; FAX: (313) 769-8383
Toll-free order line: 1 (800) 530-WORD